Sensational **Patchwork** Quilting

Marilynn Wiebe

Sterling Publishing Co., Inc. New York
A Sterling/Tamos Book

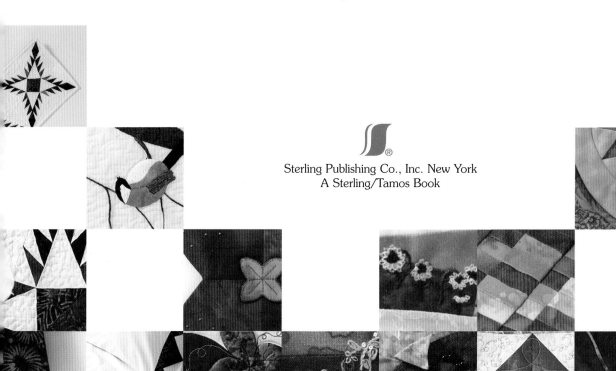

A Sterling/Tamos Book
Copyright © 2007 Marilynn Wiebe

Sterling Publishing Co., Inc.
387 Park Avenue South, New York, NY 10016-8810

Tamos Books Inc.
300 Wales Avenue, Winnipeg, MB Canada R2M 2S9

10 9 8 7 6 5 4 3 2 1

Distributed in Canada by Sterling Publishing
C/o Canadian Manda Group, 165 Dufferin Street
Toronto, Ontario, Canada M6K 3H6
Distributed in the United Kingdom by GMC Distribution Services
Castle Place, 166 High Street, Lewes, East Sussex, England BN7 1XU
Distributed in Australia by Capricorn Link (Australia) Pty. Ltd.
P.O. Box 704, Windsor, NSW 2756, Australia

Design Alice Crawford & S. Fraser
Photography Jerry Grajewski, grajewski·fotograph·inc.

Library and Archives Canada Cataloging in Publication

Wiebe, Marilynn, 1952-
        Sensational patchwork quilting / Marilynn Wiebe.

A Sterling/Tamos Book
Includes index.
ISBN-13: 978-1-895569-73-5
ISBN-10: 1-895569-73-7

        1.Patchwork--Patterns. 2. Quilting--Patterns. 3. Patchwork
quilts. I. Title. II. Title: Patchwork quilting.

TT835.W528 2007 746.46'041   C2006-904673-5

Library of Congress Cataloging-in-Publication Data Available

Tamos Books Inc. acknowledges the financial support of the Government of Canada through the Book Publishing Development Program (BPIDP) for our publishing activities.

The Authors as well as the Publisher have carefully checked the advice and directions given in this book, prior to printing. Nevertheless, no guarantee can be given as to project outcome due to individual skill levels and the possible differences in materials and tools. The Author and the Publishers will not be responsible for the results.

Acknowledgements
Machine Quilting for *Harvest Stars* done by Lynne's Custom Quilting, Lynne Langin, 177 Tupelo Avenue, Winnipeg, Manitoba, Canada, R2K 3T7 (204) 661-2866 e-mail lynnelangin@shaw.ca and Machine Quilting for *Strawberry Fields and Colors of Summer* by Cyrious Custom Quiltery, Alice Cyr, Box 19, Grp 71, R.R.#1, Anola, Manitoba, Canada, R0E 0A0 e-mail cyrbrico@mts.net

Printed in China

ISBN-13: 978-1-895569-73-5
ISBN-10: 1-895569-73-7

For information about custom editions, special sales, premium and corporate purchases, please contact Sterling Special Sales Department at 800-805-5489 or specialsales@sterlingpub.com.

About Marilynn

Photograph by Josie Avery, Wpg, MB, Canada

Marilynn lives in the heart of the Pembina Valley, Manitoba, Canada, with her husband Henry, her beloved dogs Sadie and Cochese, and three cats, surrounded by nature. She is an avid quilter and designer and has taken many prizes and awards for her quilts and unique designs and patterns. She is a sought-after judge of quilting shows and has taught a large number of quilting students over the past 20 years. Her studio is a mecca for quilters and a place to share ideas and develop new techniques, hence its name, Shared Threads. Marilynn invites all her many quilting friends to share this book and hopes to encourage new friends through the quilting on these pages.

I dedicate this book
- to my husband, Henry, who encourages me to follow my dreams, and has the patience and understanding of a saint;
- to my grandmother, Aganetha, for teaching me to love needle and thread, my mother, Katharina, for my love of gardening and attention to detail, and my daughter, Laurie-Ellen, who continues the journey;
- to all my quilting students who give me more than they will ever know, and have now become my dear friends.

Table of Contents

Patchwork Quilting

A Quieter Time

Celebration of the Wild Prairie Rose

The craft of quilting, born of necessity, has transcended its humble beginnings and risen to artistic heights. In Europe it obtained the stature of a minor art in the 14th century and reached its height of popularity from the 17th century through the 19th century. Most people, however, are familiar with quilting from the Victorian era, also know as Victorian Crazy Patchwork. These quilts were made from fine clothing fabrics such as taffetas, velvets, and silks and pieced together in a way that allowed large areas to be heavily embellished with embroidery depicting images that were dear to the quilt maker. Each quilter prided herself on the pattern design achieved and the number of different stitches used in each quilt. An example of this technique is found in Autumn Memories, p101 and the Stitcher's Companion, p104.

Not all quilts were as elaborate as Victorian crazy quilts. In many instances, necessity demanded that bedcovers be more practical, so along came cotton patchwork quilts. The pieces making up the outer layers were joined together as patchwork in quite random ways or in a simple pattern and were usually applied to a white muslin foundation. The design was completed by the quilting itself which often echoed the shape of the patchwork pattern. This style is of American origin and was distinctive in the 19th century. These practical quilts were usually made from fabric scraps at hand, pieced together in easy geometric shapes. Sometimes variations were created by making a square from nine equal parts to create a nine-patch block or units were divided into triangles to create other basic patterns. This was the beginning of a new era of quilt making, allowing all colors and shapes of scraps to be used in the quilt tops.

In rural North America in the 19th century quilting bees were popular. Women would gather, secure the layers of a quilt to the poles of a quilting frame, and sit around the edges of the frame and stitch the layers of fabric to quilt them together. This was a social event and women enjoyed getting together to share family news, pattern ideas, child rearing methods, and cooking recipes as well as making the quilt, which was a necessity for every household.

Today, the patchwork quilter borrows from all traditions to make very modern patterns and designs, such as the Double Wedding Ring which I have turned into Strawberry Fields, p49, the Burr Oak into Ice Crystals, p22, and the Churn Dash into Colors of Summer, p73. I learned the art of needlework at my grandmother's knee and it is still one of my most cherished memories. I began as a traditional quilter using patterns such as Log Cabin and Rail Fence that were available in books and magazines that I found in the public library. From these basic designs I learned and practiced all the special techniques and rules of established quilting. Quilting had guidelines and order which I appreciated and understood.

Gradually I made my own designs and patterns, and through trial and error I learned new

Photograph Josie Avery Winnipeg, MB, Canada

techniques to accommodate them. I have always admired quilts with uneven edges which allow the design to flow to the edge of the quilt and I do this in the Double Wedding Ring quilt. This quilt led me to further experiment with all my patchwork designs to find ways to have the design continue rather than come to an abrupt stop with a straight border. In this book I share with you these methods and hints to help you in your creative quilting journey. Most of what I learned in the beginning I still use, but with a new freedom to take the basic concepts and manipulate some part or sections of a pattern to create my very own design or creation. These guidelines have stayed with me and I am sharing them with you to help you establish your own creative guidelines.

Teaching quilting classes for the last twenty years has allowed me to share what I have learned, and to appreciate how the lives of all quilters are intertwined. We express ourselves creatively through our quilts, hoping to leave a legacy for the next generation. This is the common thread that ties us all together; hence, my studio is called Shared Threads.

My quilt making has always been influenced by my surroundings and special interests such as gardening, baking, entertaining, rug hooking, and every kind of needlework, and it is evident that these images and textures find their way into my quilts. From patchwork to appliqué, embellishment with exotic threads and beads, you will find quilted projects in these pages in a myriad of patterns and techniques, set out for four seasons of color. Each section includes a number of projects suitable for that season. Some of the projects are more difficult but each pattern provides complete instructions and diagrams.

Autumn Memories

Equipment needed

These are some of the basic supplies needed to create the projects in this book.

Fabric   The majority of fabrics used in this book are 100% cotton. A few specialty fabrics are used, such as velvet, taffeta, and laces. As a personal preference, I prewash all cotton fabrics to eliminate color bleeding and shrinkage.

Cutting tools   A large rotary cutter is used for cutting strips and multiple layers. A small rotary cutter is useful for trimming small pieces. A cutting mat must be used to protect the work surface as well as the cutter. I use at least two pairs of fabric scissors: a large pair for cutting fabric, a smaller pair with a sharp point for clipping, and I keep an additional pair for cutting paper and template plastic.

Note   You can label scissors so they are always used for the intended purpose.

Rulers   There are a large variety of acrylic rulers. My favorites are 8 in by 24 in, marked with 30, 45, and 60 degree angles, a 6 in by 6 in square, and a 15 in by 15 in square. Other rulers used for trimming foundation paper piecing are an Add-An Eighth and Add-A-Quarter.

Marking tools   I use white and silver chalk marking pencils, .05 mechanical pencils with leads specifically made for marking fabric, chalk wheels with white, yellow, or blue chalk, .01 Pigma pen, and ¼ in masking tape. These are just a few of the many marking tools available.

Note   The most important thing to remember when marking fabric is to check that it can be easily erased using a fabric eraser or by washing out the marks as described by the product labels.

Sewing machine   It is important to maintain your sewing machine according to the manual. Check that the stitches are locked securely between the layers of fabric being stitched. Using a straight stitch throat plate will make machine piecing easier because the pieces of fabric will not be pulled down into the machine, allowing for a pucker free seam. A ¼ in pressure foot makes piecing easier and more accurate since the finished sizes of all quilting pieces depend on the seam allowance being ¼ in. For machine quilting you will also need a walking foot, a darning foot/free motion or embroidery foot, a cover for the feed dogs or the ability to lower the feed dogs. It is also very helpful to have a large table to support the weight of the quilt as you sew.

Note   Change the sewing machine needle when starting a new project or after a few hours of stitching.

Sewing needles   For hand piecing and quilting, I prefer needles called "betweens" or quilting needles. They come in many sizes (my favorite is #11 or #12). Generally, the betweens come in #7 to # 12 (higher numbers mean smaller needles). For embroidery, purchase a package with a variety of sizes to accommodate different weights of thread. As well, I used a double-eyed embroidery needle for some of the lazy daisy stitches. For machine piecing I recommend using 80/12, and for foundation paper piecing 90/14. For machine quilting, purchase needles specifically made for that purpose. They come in a variety of sizes. For basting quilt layers together, I use a long, sharp needle.

Threads   For machine piecing I use 50 weight cotton thread in neutral colors, (cream and light gray). For hand embroidery, assemble a selection of embroidery flosses, including over dyed threads, #8 Perle cottons, rayons, and metallics. There are so many beautiful threads available in stitchery shops that are all worth experimenting with. For hand appliqué I use a cotton thread that is the same color as the appliqué shape or one shade darker if an exact match cannot be found. Silk threads can also be used for hand appliqué. You can purchase fewer colors because they blend well. Quilting thread for hand quilting is generally a little thicker and stronger than regular sewing thread and comes in a variety of colors. For machine quilting, I use #50 weight thread in the top and bottom.

Pressing A good iron and ironing board for pressing seams ensures accurate piecing. A small wooden presser or Hera marker are great tools for pressing short seams for foundation paper piecing.

Sandpaper board This is a fine sheet of sandpaper glued to the inside of a file folder. It can be used to hold fabric and templates in place allowing you to trace accurately. A sturdy sheet of cardboard or particle board could also be used instead of a file folder, making the sandpaper board into a lap board as well.

Pins Use smaller glass headed straight pins for hand appliqué and piecing. For machine piecing, I use flat flower headed pins which sit very tight against the fabric, allowing for more accurate pinning and piecing.

Note When machine piecing, remove each pin as you come to it.

Thimbles For hand quilting, I use a metal thimble that has a small ridge around the crown to prevent the needle from slipping. I also cut the finger tips off rubber gloves, and use them on my thumb for hand quilting. The rubber tip acts as a gripper to help pull the needle through the layers of the quilt. For appliqué I prefer to use leather adhesive pads that stick to your finger and are reusable. There are also a variety of leather thimbles available that are all worth trying. For machine quilting you might find that using gardening gloves that have rubber grips at the finger tips will be helpful in moving the quilt as you stitch.

Note When first learning to quilt, I went through many different kinds and shapes of thimbles until I found one that I love. Keep looking and trying to find the thimble that is right for you.

Batting There are many different types of batting available. For the projects in this book, I chose 100% cotton batting by Heirloom. I find this particular batting easy to work with for both hand and machine work. There is just enough loft to the batting to give the quilted piece dimension and still allow the piece to lie or hang flat. If a higher loft is what you hope to achieve, you may want to try polyester or polyester-cotton batting. For stuffing cushions, I used polyester fiberfill.

Note Always read the manufacturer's instructions for care of the batting and how closely the batting should be quilted. This information is vital to the finished results of your quilt.

Miscellaneous items Use a bodkin for threading ribbon ties through channels, an awl to hold fabric together as you machine piece, a seam ripper for removing stitches, a fray check for hand appliqué to seal the fabric edge when clipped, (also spray starch), white Reynolds freezer paper and template plastic for making templates, a quilting hoop for hand quilting, an embroidery hoop, round wooden toothpicks (used for needle-turned appliqué), ¼ in wide metal bias pressing bar, a regular metal teaspoon (used for hand basting quilt layers) and a box or container to hold all your necessary items so they are always where you want them to be.

How-to Techniques

Fabric preparation

Purchase the best quality 100% cotton available. To help prevent colors from running or fabrics becoming uneven with shrinkage, I prewash fabrics. In some patterns it is important to position the edge of one side of the template on a grain line — either selvage to selvage, which is the crosswise grain and has a slight stretch, or parallel to selvage, which is the lengthwise grain and has no stretch. Corner to opposite corner is the diagonal grain or bias and is very stretchy.

 Note Be sure not to include the selvage edges in any part of your quilt.

Batting

Choice of batting greatly influences the appearance of the quilt. Cotton or cotton/polyester blends reduce the chance of tucks and pleats because the quilt top clings to the batting. After being washed this batting becomes very soft and drapes well. Wool is also soft and lightweight with high loft. Choose it if a lot of close quilting is required because it will not become stiff.

Making templates

Position template plastic or white freezer paper (shiny side down) on top of the pattern in the book. Using a fine point permanent marking pen and a ruler for all straight lines, trace outline accurately. Add all information to the template as it appears, including any special reference marks or lines.

Using templates

For appliqué, position plastic templates on right side of fabric, leaving a space (seam allowance) between each template. If using freezer paper templates, place the shiny side down and iron (try medium setting).Then place the appliqué fabric with the ironed-on templates onto the sandpaper board. Trace around the templates with an appropriate marking tool. The sandpaper will hold the fabric in place allowing you to trace accurately.

 Note Appliqué templates should be placed on the fabric with as many edges as possible on the diagonal grain of the fabric. Bias edges are easier to turn under than edges placed on the straight of grain.

 Note After all templates are traced, cut them out roughly, leaving a generous seam allowance and stack them in numerical order. This makes it easier to keep all pieces organized.

Hand piecing

Using a marking tool, trace a fine line around templates on the wrong side of the fabric. Cut out, allowing ¼ in seam allowance around pieces. Following your design, take the first two pieces, place right sides together, and pin on the drawn line using small straight pins. With neutral colored thread and small needle, take a small stitch at the beginning of the seam on the drawn line, and backstitch on the same first stitch to secure (backstitches replace knot which leaves a lump on the stitched line). Continue sewing with a small running stitch, staying on the line on both pieces. Once you reach the end of the seam (end of the pencil line), end off by making two backstitches on top of the last stitch and leave a ¼ in tail of thread and cut. Continue in this manner until all pieces are stitched together.

Abbreviations used on diagrams

r.s.t.— right side together
s.a. — seam allowance
w.s. — wrong side
m.s. — machine stitch
w.o.f. — width of fabric

Rotary cutting

This method is used for cutting strips and sub-cuts for machine piecing. Measurements include ¼ in seam allowance.

1 Fold fabric in half lengthwise matching selvages and aligning crosswise and lengthwise grains. Place folded edge closest to you on cutting mat and align a square ruler along folded edge of fabric.

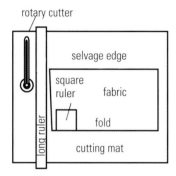

2 Place a long ruler to the left of the square ruler making sure that the raw edges of the fabric on the left side are covered.

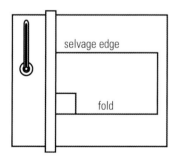

3 Remove square ruler and cut along the right side of the long ruler starting from the folded fabric edge. Push all the cotton away from you. Cut to where your fingers are anchoring the ruler and leave the cutter in the fabric. Walk your hand up the ruler and continue to cut the complete strip. Discard the cut-off strip. You now have a perfectly square piece of fabric.

 Note Reverse these directions if you are left-handed.

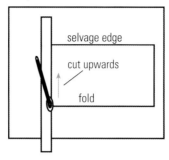

4 Position the long ruler on the newly cut edge of fabric. With the ruler mark the required width of strips and cut.

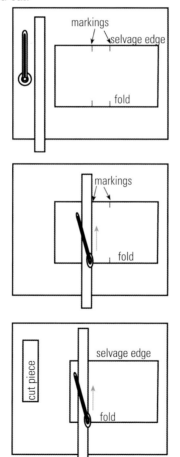

5 To make subcuts, place the strip on the cutting board, trim off the selvage, cut the required size pieces.

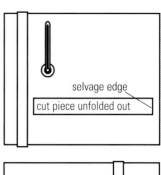

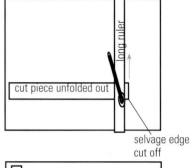

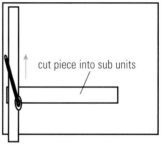

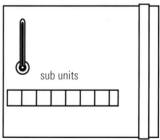

Basting

Prior to quilting, whether by hand or machine, the three layers of a quilt (quilt top, batting, and backing) need to be basted using quilter's safety pins, or needle and thread. I prefer the old-fashioned needle and thread.

1 Secure the backing to a table or other flat surface by taping the edges. Backing fabric is right side down.

2 Lay batting on top, smoothing it out.

3 Place quilt top on batting, making sure to have about the same amount of batting and backing extending beyond the quilt top.

4 Using white or off white thread, never colored, and a longer needle, start basting from the center out to the edges.

 Note I try to baste in 2 in to 4 in grids. This takes a lot of time, but I like the security of knowing that nothing will shift. When hand quilting a large quilt I also wrap the backing over the batting, bringing it to the front and stitching it in place. This keeps the batting from shredding at the edges.

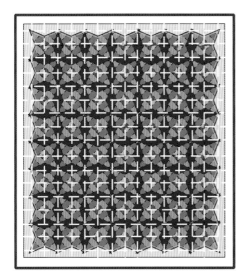

backing, batting, and quilt top

 Note Alternatively, use brass safety pins for basting (approx. 5 – 6 hundred for a queen size quilt), or a basting spray which is a temporary adhesive that washes out. A quilt tack is a plastic tab tacking system that has a needle-like device.

Machine piecing

The most important thing to remember is to establish an exact ¼ in inside seam allowance. You could do this by using a special quilting foot that measures ¼ in from the needle to the edge of the foot, or by securing a guideline on the needle plate with masking tape.

 Note To make sure that the seam allowance is correct cut 3 pieces of fabric measuring 1 in wide x approximately 4 in. Sew these strips together and press. The middle piece must measure ½ in wide. If not, adjust seam allowance.

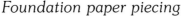

Foundation paper piecing

Foundation piecing has been used for many years and can be traced back to quilts that were first pieced onto a fabric foundation. A more recent development to foundation piecing is using paper that is somewhat transparent. Photocopy the required number of paper piece patterns. These paper patterns are numbered and the numbers are followed numerically for piecing.

1 Set the stitch length of sewing machine to approximately 18 stitches per inch. This short stitch will perforate the paper and allow for easier removal later. I use a $^{19}/_{14}$ size needle and a thread that blends with the colors of the project.

2 Place the fabric for piece #1 right side up on the unmarked side of the paper, making sure the fabric is large enough to cover the area marked #1 and extend beyond the lines on all sides. If the piece is too small cut a larger one. The excess can always be trimmed later. Place fabric piece for

#2 on top of fabric piece #1, seam allowance together along the joining seam, which is the line between #1 and #2, lining up the edges at the seam line.

3 Sew these first 2 fabric pieces onto the foundation along the sewing line between #1 and #2, extending the stitches a little beyond the beginning and the end of the line.

 Note Remember that you are sewing with fabric underneath the paper and the sewing lines on top. This seems strange at first since everything seems backwards.

4 Trim away any excess fabric in the seam allowance to either ⅛ in or ¼ in by folding back the paper foundation on stitched line. Place add-an-eighth or add-a-quarter ruler on pieced unit and trim.

5 Press piece #2 open. You will now have covered pieces #1 and #2.

6 Add piece #3 and so on, until outline unit is sewn.

7 Trim the outer edge of the paper foundation piece so that you have an accurate ¼ in seam allowance. See Ice Crystals quilt p22 for detailed diagrams.

Appliqué

This is the layering of fabric onto a background piece to create a pattern design. Appliqué can be worked by hand or machine with various ways to prepare the edges. The background fabric needs to be marked with placement lines to identify where each piece will fit. Alternatively you can trace the design onto tracing paper or vinyl to use as an overlay. This eliminates marking the background fabric.

Hand appliqué

Example (needle-trim method with design traced on fabric for placement guide, using a marking tool that is easily removed).

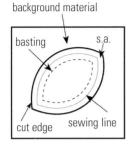

1 Trim appliqué shape to ⅛ in seam allowance. Position on background using small pins to secure or baste shape in place ¼ in inside the marked stitching line.

2 Make a tiny knot at the end of the thread, using thread color that matches the appliqué shape. Insert the needle into the appliqué shape coming up on the stitching line. The knot will be on the underside of the appliqué shape.

3 Using the needle or round wood toothpick, turn seam allowance under up to marked stitching line. Insert the needle into the background fabric just behind where the thread emerges at the fabric fold and take a tiny stitch. Keeping the needle parallel to the appliqué edge, bring the tip of the needle into the fold of appliqué shape.

 Note An appliqué stitch is a series of very tiny invisible stitches.

Fusible appliqué

This method of appliqué uses a fusible appliqué film. There are a number of different brands and all work well, but the lightweight products are best suited for small appliqué pieces. These products have a shiny sticky side and a paper side. The paper side is the side the pattern is traced onto. This product is easy to see through, so allows for easy tracing of pattern.

1 Trace pattern onto paper side, cut out leaving a narrow margin of paper around the traced edge of design.

2 Iron cut-out shapes onto the wrong side of the fabric, using a dry iron. Follow manufacturer's instructions for heat temperature and duration of pressing.

3 Cut out the pattern shape on the drawn line. Peel the paper off the pattern piece. Iron onto the appropriate section of the appliqué project right side of fabric. These appliqué pieces are now considered to be complete, but I prefer to finish the edges with a tiny row of blanket stitch embroidery using embroidery floss that matches the appliqué fabric.

Stems

Finished width is ¼ in wide. For all methods cut a ¾ in wide bias strip at a 45° angle approximately 20 in long.

cut at 45° angle for bias

Method 1

1 Cut ¾ in bias strips.

2 Fold into thirds, wrong sides together, and baste.

3 Pin to background. Appliqué inside curve first.

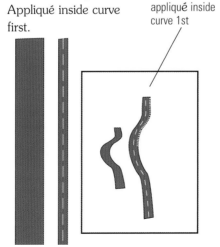

appliqué inside curve 1st

Method 2

1 Cut ¾ in wide bias strip.

2 Fold in half lengthwise, wrong sides together.

3 Stitch in place with a small running stitch, inside curve first, through all thicknesses approximately ⅛ in from raw edge of folded stem.

4 Flip stem over top of stitching, and appliqué the folded side in place.

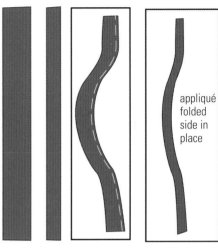

appliqué folded side in place

Method 3

1 Cut ¾ in bias strips. Bring the two edges of the cut strips together and sew very close to edge with a fine stitch on the sewing machine.

2 Insert ¼ in wide bias pressing bar and press with a hot iron, making a sharp crease on both sides.

3 Position in place and remember to stitch the inside curve first.

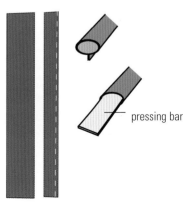

pressing bar

Points

1 Start stitching about ½ in down from tip on right side of leaf. (Left handed, start stitching on left side.)
2 Stitch up to tip of leaf. Trim off excess seam allowance that extends beyond left seam allowance.
3 Turn top seam allowance straight across. Take 1 more stitch extending just beyond the tip of leaf.
4 Tuck under the seam allowance on the left side with pin or needle.
5 Now appliqué down the left side. The extra elongated stitch that you made at the top of the leaf will act as an optical illusion making your point look very sharp.

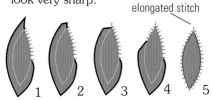

elongated stitch

1　2　3　4　5

Vs / Cleavages / Outside curves

1 Prepare inside Vs with a very small drop of fray check (place small amount onto a plastic lid and use tip of toothpick to dab on fabric). Let dry.
2 Trim seam allowance, clip into Vs.
3 Position and stitch, starting at the top of a rounded petal.
4 Fold next petal completely under the appliqué shape and stitch down into the V or cleavage.
5 Untuck flower petal, and continue to stitch in this manner all the way around the flower making sure to tuck each petal under as you near the V.

Note When stitching outside curves, make sure to trim the seam allowance to about ⅛ in. This will make a nice smooth line rather than a bunched up seam allowance that causes points to occur.

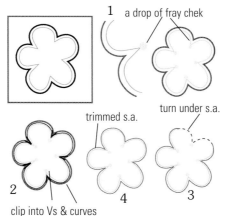

1　a drop of fray chek

trimmed s.a.

turn under s.a.

2　4　3

clip into Vs & curves

Inside Curves

Make sure to feather clip inside curves. This will make it easier to turn under seam allowance smoothly. Using a wooden toothpick will make turning easier.

feather clip inside curve

Circles/Berries

For circles up to ¾ in diameter.
1 Make a freezer paper template for the size you need. You will need one paper circle for each fabric circle.
2 Place freezer paper circle on the wrong side of fabric and iron on. Cut out leaving a generous ¼ in seam allowance.
3 Using thread that matches appliqué fabric, run a gathering stitch just inside the cut edge of fabric starting with a knot on the inside and ending with the thread on the right side. Make these stitches small and even.
4 Pull thread up tightly, gathering the fabric around the circle.
5 Appliqué in place using the same thread.
6 Cut a small x in the background and remove the paper.

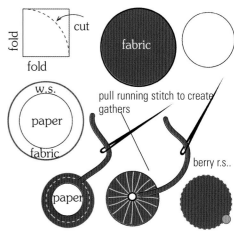

fold　cut

fold

fabric

w.s.

paper

fabric

pull running stitch to create gathers

paper

berry r.s..

Large circles

1 Make a cardboard or non-melting plastic circle the size that you need.
2 Cut a fabric circle at least ¼ in larger than template.
3 Using a matching thread, place a running stitch all the way around. Pull gathers tightly and press with hot iron using spray starch to set.
4 Remove template and stitch in place.

Quilting by hand

Place the quilt in the hoop making sure that the quilt is not too taut. Generally you begin to quilt in the center and work to the outer edge.
1 Using a single strand of thread about 18 in–20 in long make a small knot at the end of thread.
2 Begin quilting by inserting needle into the quilt top about ½–¾ in away from where the first stitch will start. Bring the needle through the top and batting only. Come up at the spot where 1st stitch begins. Pull thread and tug it to pop the knot through the top so that it is buried between the layers.
3 The quilting stitch is a running stitch that must go through all 3 layers.

running stitch

4 With a thimble on your middle finger, insert the needle straight down one stitch length from where thread is located. Using the thimble push needle through the layers until you can barely feel it on your index finger of your left (underneath) hand.

5 Using the thimble rock the eye of the needle down while at the same time the underneath finger is pushing up to bring the needle tip back to the surface.

6 Using the thumb of the sewing hand, depress the quilt just ahead of the needle point, thus helping to push the quilt onto the needle tip. This is the 1st stitch. You can pull the thread through after each stitch or leave several stitches on the needle and then pull the thread through. The stitches should be fairly snug to show dimpling but not so tight that the quilt is distorted.

7 To end thread, wrap thread around needle and guide knot down to quilt top. Pop knot under quilt top by going into the same hole as the last stitch.

Note Practice first to focus on technique and then try to make stitches smaller and even.

Quilting by machine

If you choose to quilt by machine you must have a sewing machine large enough for big quilts. Consult books and articles for instruction in this process. Alternatively, you can have the quilting done by a professional machine quilter in your area.

Making binding

1 To make double-fold binding with mitered corners, first determine the width of binding needed for your piece. For a finished ¼ in wide binding cut 2 in wide strips. For ⅜ in wide binding cut 2½ in wide strips. For ½ in wide binding cut 3 in wide strips.

2 Cut strips across width of fabric, selvage to selvage. To determine number of strips needed, measure the perimeter of your quilt and add approximately 40 in. For example, 240 in plus 40 in = 280 in. Most strips measure 40 in long so 280 in divide by 40 in = 7 strips or 8 strips to be on the safe side.

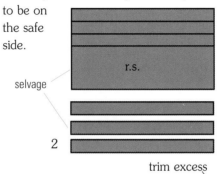

r.s.

selvage

2

3 Sew those strips together, end to end. To join the strips place one strip right side up on work space and place second strip right side down on top of bottom strip, perpendicular to it.

4 Draw a stitching line diagonally with a ruler. Pin strips together and sew on line. Trim away excess fabric ¼ in beyond stitching.

5 Repeat this process until you have all strips joined together.

6 Fold binding in half lengthwise and press wrong side together.

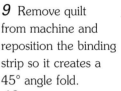

trim excess

3

4

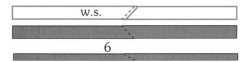

w.s.

6

Attaching binding

7 Place quilt right side up next to sewing machine. The quilt will still have all the extra batting and backing extending beyond the quilt top.

8 With the raw edges of the binding and raw edge of the quilt top even, position the binding on top, near the middle of one side. Leave approximately the first 7 in of the binding unstitched and begin sewing ¼ in seam, sewing to within ¼ in from the corner. Stop with a few backstitches.

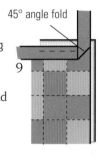

backstitch

8

45° angle fold

9

9 Remove quilt from machine and reposition the binding strip so it creates a 45° angle fold.

10 Bring binding fold back down along the next side to be stitched, creating a 90° angle fold at the top.

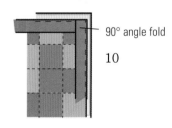

90° angle fold

10

11 Start sewing at the top and repeat the mitering at each corner. Stop stitching approximately 7 in from the point where you started.

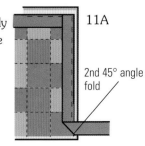

11A

2nd 45° angle fold

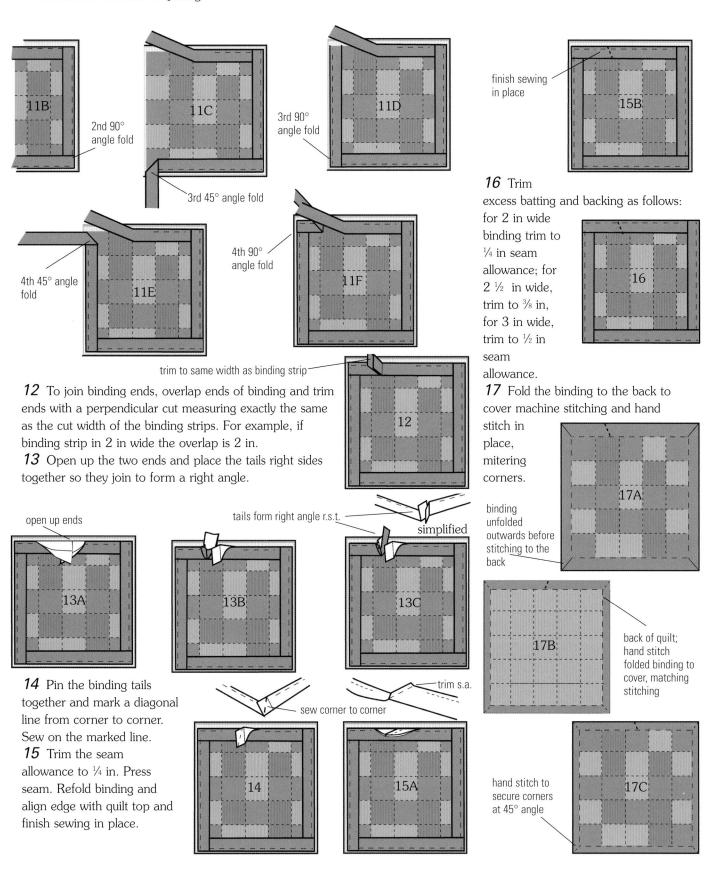

11B

2nd 90°
angle fold

11C

3rd 90°
angle fold

3rd 45° angle fold

11D

finish sewing
in place

15B

4th 45° angle
fold

11E

4th 90°
angle fold

11F

16 Trim
excess batting and backing as follows:
for 2 in wide
binding trim to
¼ in seam
allowance; for
2 ½ in wide,
trim to ⅜ in,
for 3 in wide,
trim to ½ in
seam
allowance.

16

trim to same width as binding strip

12 To join binding ends, overlap ends of binding and trim
ends with a perpendicular cut measuring exactly the same
as the cut width of the binding strips. For example, if
binding strip in 2 in wide the overlap is 2 in.

13 Open up the two ends and place the tails right sides
together so they join to form a right angle.

12

17 Fold the binding to the back to
cover machine stitching and hand
stitch in
place,
mitering
corners.

17A

binding
unfolded
outwards before
stitching to the
back

open up ends

tails form right angle r.s.t.

simplified

13A

13B

13C

back of quilt;
hand stitch
folded binding to
cover, matching
stitching

17B

14 Pin the binding tails
together and mark a diagonal
line from corner to corner.
Sew on the marked line.

15 Trim the seam
allowance to ¼ in. Press
seam. Refold binding and
align edge with quilt top and
finish sewing in place.

sew corner to corner

trim s.a.

14

15A

hand stitch to
secure corners
at 45° angle

17C

Binding uneven edges

1 Prepare binding as for straight edges. For curved corners prepare binding by cutting on the bias. Begin sewing up from a corner (outside or inside). Make a dot at each inside corner ¼ in from corner.

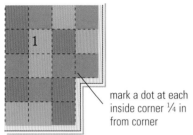

mark a dot at each inside corner ¼ in from corner

2 Place prepared binding on top of quilt (for outside corner see Making Binding section p13) and sew ¼ in seam allowance.

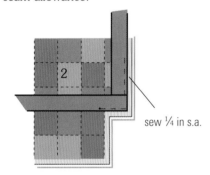

sew ¼ in s.a.

3 Sew up to ¼ in from corner (up to dot), backstitch and sew back to the dot, stopping with needle down.

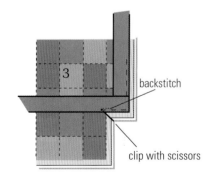

backstitch

clip with scissors

4 Lift the pressure foot; using small sharp scissors clip diagonally into the inside corner through quilt top,

batting, and backing. This will enable you to straighten the edge of the quilt.

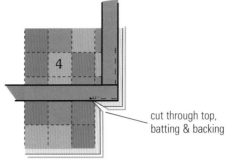

cut through top, batting & backing

5 Sew a few stitches and backstitch, then sew to the next corner. Repeat until entire quilt is bound.

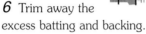

straighten quilt & sew few stitches & backstitch before sewing to next corner

6 Trim away the excess batting and backing.

7 Turn binding to the back and hand stitch the folded edge of the binding in place covering the machine stitching line.

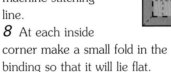

8 At each inside corner make a small fold in the binding so that it will lie flat.

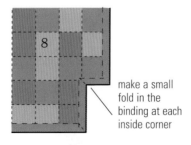

make a small fold in the binding at each inside corner

Hanging sleeve

If you plan to hang your quilts, you may wish to add a rod pocket or hanging sleeve. I generally use leftover backing fabric for this.

1 Cut a strip about 6 in wide by the width of your quilt and hem both ends by turning under about ½ in at each end.

turn under ends & hem

2 Fold fabric strip in half lengthwise, width sides together.

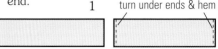

3 Baste top edge (raw edge) to the top of quilt back. The top edge can then be secured with the binding.

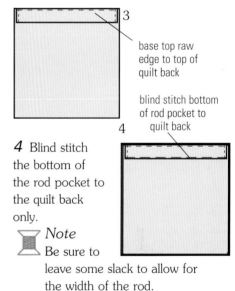

base top raw edge to top of quilt back

blind stitch bottom of rod pocket to quilt back

4 Blind stitch the bottom of the rod pocket to the quilt back only.

Note
Be sure to leave some slack to allow for the width of the rod.

Finishing label

Sign and date all your work. This could be something as simple as placing your initials and the date in the bottom right hand corner or making an elaborate label copyright with an acid-free pen or hand embroidery. The label should include your full name, the quilt name, date, and any other information that would relate to the quilter or to the recipient.

Basic embroidery stitches

These basic embroidery stitches are used in the projects in this book.

Basic Embroidery Stitches

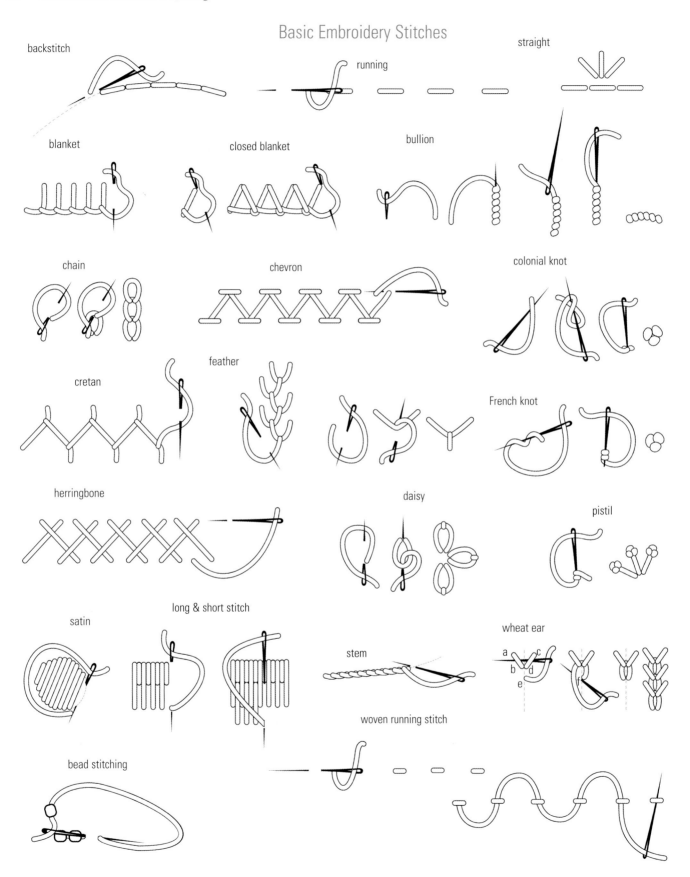

backstitch

running

straight

blanket

closed blanket

bullion

chain

chevron

colonial knot

cretan

feather

French knot

herringbone

daisy

pistil

satin

long & short stitch

stem

wheat ear

woven running stitch

bead stitching

1 Cut 4 strips 2¼ in x width of fabric and cross cut strips into 128 pieces 1¼ in x 2¼ in. Label this pile W1.

2 Cut 16 strips 2¾ in x width of fabric and cross cut 8 of these strips into 256 pieces 1 in x 2¾ in. Label this pile W2. Cross cut the remaining 8 strips into 256 pieces 1¼ in x 2¾ in. Label this pile W3.

3 Cut 15 strips 2¼ in x width of fabric and cross cut into 384 pieces 1½ in x 2¼ in. Label this pile W4.

4 From blue/purple fabrics

Color A Cut 5 strips 2¼ in x width of fabric and cross cut strips into 128 pieces 1½ in x 2¼ in. Label ths pile A1. Cut 4 strips 2½ in x width of fabric and cross cut strips into 128 pieces 1 in x 2½ in. Label this pile A2.

Color B Cut 5 strips 2¼ in x width of fabric and cross cut strips into 128 pieces 1½ in x 2¼ in. Label this pile B1. Cut 4 strips 2½ in x width of fabric and cross cut strips into 128 pieces 1 in x 2½ in. Label this pile B2.

Color C Cut 5 strips 2¼ in x width of fabric and cross cut strips into 128 pieces 1½ in x 2¼ in. Label this pile C1. Cut 4 strips 2½ in x width of fabric and cross cut strips into 128 pieces 1 in x 2½ in. Label this pile C2.

Color D Cut 5 strips 3½ in x width of fabric and cross cut strips into 128 pieces 1½ in x 3½ in. Label this pile D1. Then follow piecing instructions, pp23-24. Continue these steps for all remaining unit As (128 units). Use the same piecing method for unit B (128 units).

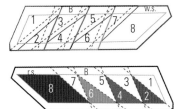

❄ Note Leave all papers attached until all units are stitched together.

Instructions for Piecing Unit A

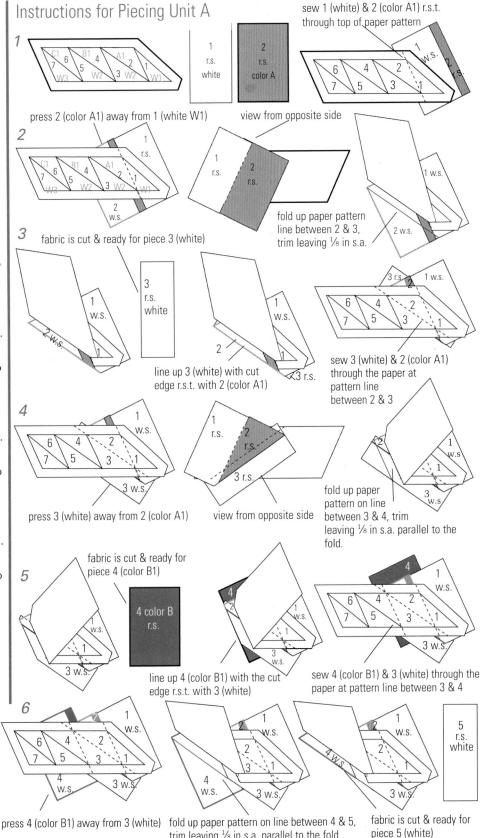

1

2 press 2 (color A1) away from 1 (white W1)

3 fabric is cut & ready for piece 3 (white)
line up 3 (white) with cut edge r.s.t. with 2 (color A1)

4 press 3 (white) away from 2 (color A1)

5 fabric is cut & ready for piece 4 (color B1)
line up 4 (color B1) with the cut edge r.s.t. with 3 (white)

6 press 4 (color B1) away from 3 (white)
fold up paper pattern on line between 4 & 5, trim leaving ⅛ in s.a. parallel to the fold.
fabric is cut & ready for piece 5 (white)

sew 1 (white) & 2 (color A1) r.s.t. through top of paper pattern

view from opposite side

fold up paper pattern line between 2 & 3, trim leaving ⅛ in s.a.

sew 3 (white) & 2 (color A1) through the paper at pattern line between 2 & 3

view from opposite side

fold up paper pattern on line between 3 & 4, trim leaving ⅛ in s.a. parallel to the fold.

sew 4 (color B1) & 3 (white) through the paper at pattern line between 3 & 4

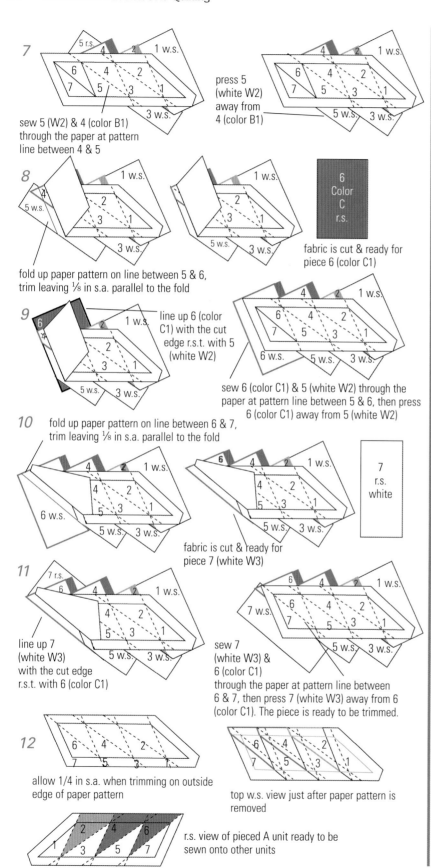

7   sew 5 (W2) & 4 (color B1) through the paper at pattern line between 4 & 5

press 5 (white W2) away from 4 (color B1)

8   fold up paper pattern on line between 5 & 6, trim leaving ⅛ in s.a. parallel to the fold

fabric is cut & ready for piece 6 (color C1)

9   line up 6 (color C1) with the cut edge r.s.t. with 5 (white W2)

sew 6 (color C1) & 5 (white W2) through the paper at pattern line between 5 & 6, then press 6 (color C1) away from 5 (white W2)

10   fold up paper pattern on line between 6 & 7, trim leaving ⅛ in s.a. parallel to the fold

fabric is cut & ready for piece 7 (white W3)

11   line up 7 (white W3) with the cut edge r.s.t. with 6 (color C1)

sew 7 (white W3) & 6 (color C1) through the paper at pattern line between 6 & 7, then press 7 (white W3) away from 6 (color C1). The piece is ready to be trimmed.

12   allow 1/4 in s.a. when trimming on outside edge of paper pattern

top w.s. view just after paper pattern is removed

r.s. view of pieced A unit ready to be sewn onto other units

5 **Cutting Unit F** Make 128 copies of unit F paper pattern (p26). Pre-cut fabric pieces for unit F as follows:

From white fabric

Cut 9 strips 3¼ in x width of fabric and cross cut these strips into 128 pieces 2¾ in x 3¼ in. Label these pieces F1

6 **From blue/purple fabric**

Color E Cut 6 strips 2¾ in x width of fabric and cross cut into 128 pieces 1¾ in x 2¾ in. Label these pieces E1.

Paper piece each Unit F using these 2 pieces. Press seam allowance towards E color.

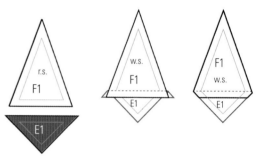

7 Unit G Use freezer paper template, includes seam allowance. Fold fabric right sides together and cut 10 strips 5¼ in x width of fabric, then cut 64 pairs of G as shown.

❄ *Note* By flipping template there is no waste.

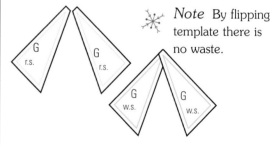

8 **Assembly Instructions** Sew unit A to side of Unit F. Sew with A on top, matching points.

diagram simplified

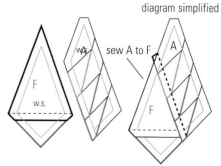

sew A to F

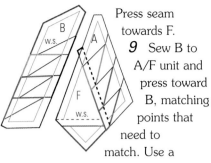

Press seam towards F.

9 Sew B to A/F unit and press toward B, matching points that need to match. Use a straight pin to help line up these key points.

10 Sew a pair of Gs to each long side of the A/B/F unit. The pieced unit should measure 5 in x 5 in see below (includes seam allowance). Make a total of 128.

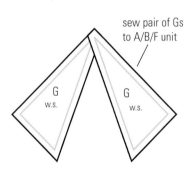

sew B to A/F

sew pair of Gs to A/B/F unit

G w.s.   G w.s.

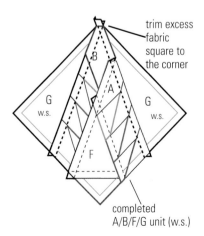

trim excess fabric square to the corner

B

G w.s.   A   G w.s.

F

completed A/B/F/G unit (w.s.)

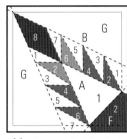

G

8
7
1
5
6
2
3
4
4
5
B
G
A
1
2
1
2
F
7
2

completed A/B/F /G unit r.s.

11 Assemble blocks by sewing 4 sections together to make 1 pattern block, as shown below.

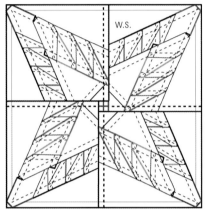

w.s.

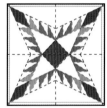

completed pattern block r.s.

12 Assemble Quilt Top by piecing in diagonal rows, as shown. Sew rows together and press. Line up corners of blocks carefully.

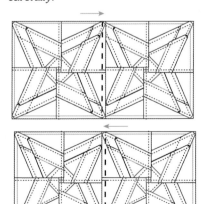

detail of seams – press blocks in direction of arrows.

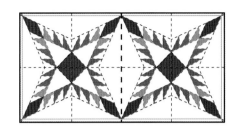

sew & press blocks in direction of arrows

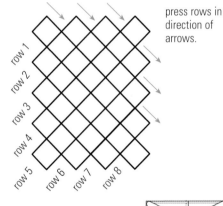

row 1
row 2
row 3
row 4
row 5
row 6
row 7
row 8

drawings simplified

press rows in direction of arrows.

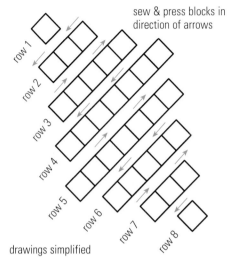

row 1
row 2
row 3
row 4
row 5
row 6
row 7
row 8

detail of stitching and row alignment of an outside edge

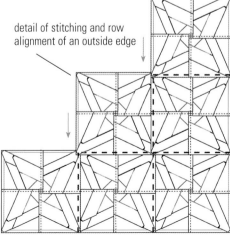

stitching & row alignment guide

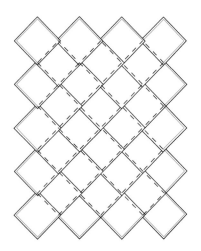

13 Layer backing/batting and quilt top. Baste layers together (see p9).

14 Quilt with loose meandering curves and swirls, representing blowing snow.

an example of quilting stitches used

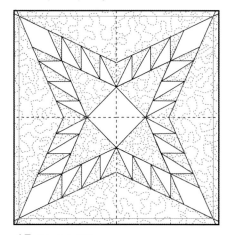

15 Bind (p13).

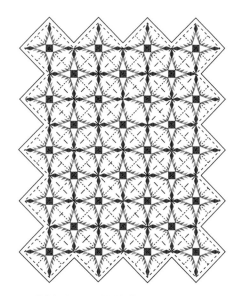

finished quilt with binding sewn on

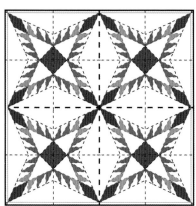

r.s. view portion of quilt top after rows are stitched together

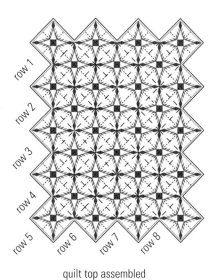

row 1
row 2
row 3
row 4
row 5   row 6   row 7   row 8

quilt top assembled

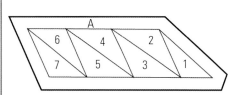

A

6   4   2
7   5   3   1

Patterns A, B, F & G
half size

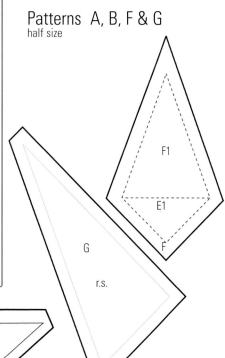

F1

E1

F

G

r.s.

B

1   3   5   7   8
2   4   6

Winter Curtain
Tie-Backs

The seasonal curtain tie-backs continue the blue/purple on icy white winter theme. Tie-back points feature purple crystal beads.

Materials
- fabric ½ yd from a
  variety of blue/purple
  colors
- beads
- 4 cabon rings (optional)

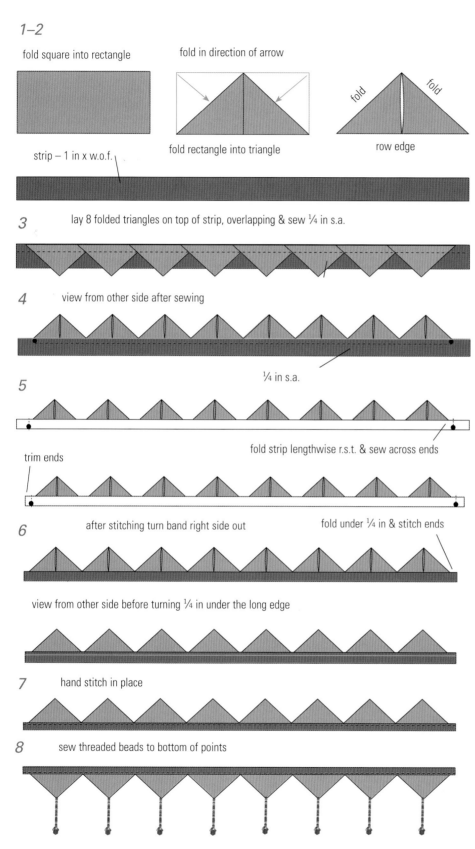

1–2

fold square into rectangle

fold in direction of arrow

fold rectangle into triangle

fold   fold

row edge

strip – 1 in x w.o.f.

3 lay 8 folded triangles on top of strip, overlapping & sew ¼ in s.a.

4 view from other side after sewing

¼ in s.a.

5

fold strip lengthwise r.s.t. & sew across ends

trim ends

6 after stitching turn band right side out

fold under ¼ in & stitch ends

view from other side before turning ¼ in under the long edge

7 hand stitch in place

8 sew threaded beads to bottom of points

Directions

1 Cut two 1 in x width of fabric strips for top band. Cut two 5 in x width of fabric pieces and cut this into sixteen 5 in x 5 in squares.

2 Fold all 5 in squares in half and press, as shown.

3 Place 1 in x width of fabric strips flat and position 8 folded triangles on each strip, overlapping, as shown, but having the row edges of folded triangles even with the edge of the strip. Make sure to leave an extension of strip on each end, as shown. Position all triangles so that the center fold faces down.

4 Sew ¼ in seam allowance Press towards the strip.

5 Fold strip in half lengthwise, right sides together, and sew across the ends even with the inside point of the triangles.

6 Turn strip right side out and fold remaining long edge under ¼ in.

7 Hand stitch in place.

8 Add threaded beads to the bottom of each triangle.

9 A cabon ring can be added to each end to secure curtain tie-backs. A cabon ring is a small plastic ring that is used in sewing curtains/drapes. These small rings are sewn to the end of each tie-back and can then be secured to window frame to pull back the curtain.

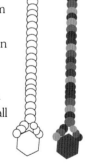

threaded beads, 26 beads & one decorative bead for each strand

Winter Bed
Linens

The seasonal bed linens decoration imitates the design of the curtain tie-backs to provide a custom look to the bedroom.

Materials

- purchased white top sheet (66 in wide) and 2 matching standard size pillowcases 19½ in across
- blue/purple for bands ¼ yd
- various fabrics for triangles ¾ yd

sew ¼ in s.a. through the band & pillowcase

3 ¼ in

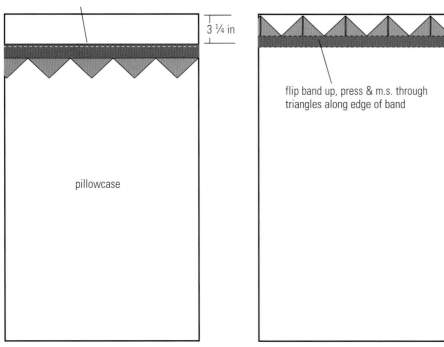

pillowcase

flip band up, press & m.s. through triangles along edge of band

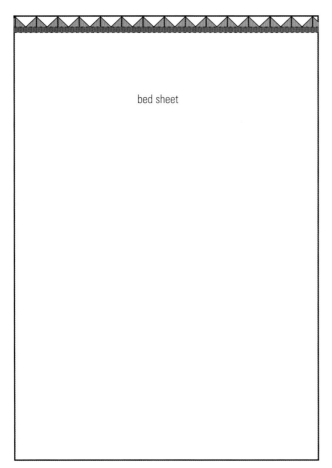

bed sheet

Directions

1 Cut four 1½ in x width of fabric strips for top bands.

2 Cut five 5 in x width of fabric pieces and cut into thirty-three 5 in x 5 in squares.

Note You will use 9 for each pillowcase and 15 for top sheet.

3 Prepare triangles in the same manner as curtain tie-backs (p 28)

4 For pillowcases, place 9 triangles on each band, overlapping in the same way as curtain tie-backs. Sew in place with ¼ in seam allowance.

5 Undo side seam of pillowcase as far down as needed.

6 With right sides together, place pieced band 3¼ in down from top edge of pillowcase. Sew ¼ in seam through the band and pillowcase.

7 Flip band up (wrong side of band to right side of pillowcase).

8 Press and stitch the band in place, carefully machine stitching through the triangles along the edge of the band.

9 Re-stitch the side seams of the pillowcases.

10 Repeat the steps for the top sheet. Join two 1½ in strips together, end to end, and trim band to measure width (undo side edges of sheet).

11 Place 15 folded triangles and proceed in the same manner as pillowcases.

12 Re-stitch side edges.

Note Seed beads could also be added to the point of each triangle.

Friendship Stars
Bolster

T his bolster pillow is an excellent additon to the winter bedroom setting. It is made from 12 pieced star blocks. The bolster measures 8 in diameter by 26 in long.

Directions: cutting pieces

1 To make outer bolster use white fabric and cut three 2½ in x width of fabric strips and cross-cut these into 2½ in x 2½ in squares. Make 48.

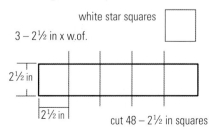

white star squares

3 – 2½ in x w.of.

2½ in

2½ in

cut 48 – 2½ in squares

2 Cut two 3 in x width of fabric strips and cross-cut these into 3 in x 3 in squares. Make 24.

white star points

2 – 3 in x w.o.f.

3 in

3 in

cut 24 – 3 in squares

Materials

- background fabric for outer cushion and fabric for cushion form white tone on tone print 1¾ yds
- cushion solid white fabric ¾ yd blue/purple fabric ¾ yd
- purple accent fabric ⅛ yd
- cotton batting 1 piece 26 in x 30 in
- 2 lb bag poly stuffing
- 312 seed beads
- 12 decorative beads
- bugle beads
- *Note* Each pieced star block measures 6 in x 6 in. Save all leftover pieces of batting for stuffing material

3 Cut two 8½ in x width of fabric strips and cut into two 8½ in x 24½ in pieces (for the ends).

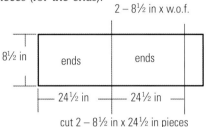

2 – 8½ in x w.o.f.

8½ in | ends | ends

24½ in — 24½ in

cut 2 – 8½ in x 24½ in pieces

4 To make inside cushion use white fabric and cut one 24 in x width of fabric strip and cross cut into a 24 in x 26 in piece. Cut two 8 in diameter circles from leftover fabric.

❄ *Note* The cushion is slightly smaller than the outer bolster.

1 – 24 in w.o.f.

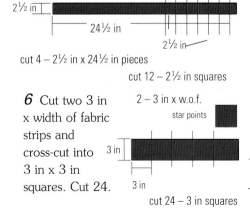

24 in | inside bolster backing | cushion

26 in

cut 2 – 8 in dia circles

5 From blue/purple fabric cut four 2½ in x width of fabric strips and cross-cut into four 2½ in x 24½ in pieces used for the bands. Cut the remaining fabric from each band into 2½ in x 2½ in star centers. Cut 12.

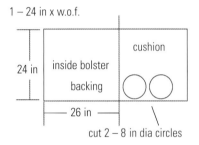

4– 2½ in x w.o.f.   bands & star squares

2½ in

24½ in

2½ in

cut 4 – 2½ in x 24½ in pieces

cut 12 – 2½ in squares

6 Cut two 3 in x width of fabric strips and cross-cut into 3 in x 3 in squares. Cut 24.

2 – 3 in x w.o.f.
star points

3 in

3 in

cut 24 – 3 in squares

7 From purple accent fabric cut two 1¼ in x width of fabric strips and cross cut into two 1¼ in x 24½ in pieces.

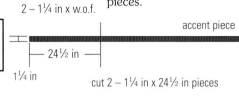

2 – 1¼ in x w.o.f.

accent piece

24½ in

1¼ in

cut 2 – 1¼ in x 24½ in pieces

Friendship Stars

Make twelve 6 in friendship stars.

1 To make star points place one 3 in white square on top of one blue/purple square, right sides together.

2 With a pencil and ruler draw a line on the white square, diagonally corner to corner.

3 Stitch ¼ in seam allowance on both sides of drawn line.

4 Cut on drawn line. Each stitched square makes two (half square triangles) star point units.

5 Press seams toward darkest fabric.

6 Repeat with remaining 3 squares to create 48 star point units.

7 Trim all star point units to measure 2½ in x 2½ in.

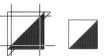

finished 2 ½ in square

❄ *Note* When trimming, be sure to have the corner edge at the stitched seam.

8 For each star block use four 2½ in x 2½ in white squares, 4 star point units, and one 2½ in x 2½ in blue/purple square.

Begin by sewing units into rows and press seams in direction of arrows. Row 1 – 1 star point, two 2½ in white squares. Row 2 – 2 star points, one 2½ in star center. Row 3 – 1 star point, two 2½ in white squares.

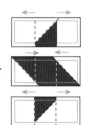

9 Sew rows together and press seams in direction of arrows. Blocks should measure 6½ in x 6½ in (includes seam allowance).

Block 1

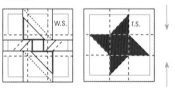

w.s.   r.s.

10 Make 6 star blocks with star points in the one direction.

11 Repeat steps 8 and 9 but change direction of star point units for the remaining 6 star blocks.

Block 2

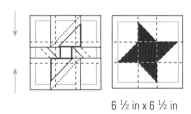

6 ½ in x 6 ½ in

12 Assemble cushion top by sewing pieced star blocks together into 3 rows of 4 blocks each. Alternate block 1 and block 2. Each row should measure 6½ in x 24½ in.

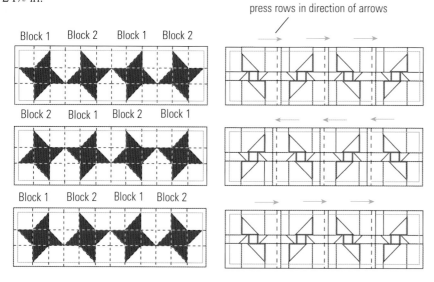

press rows in direction of arrows

Block 1   Block 2   Block 1   Block 2

Block 2   Block 1   Block 2   Block 1

Block 1   Block 2   Block 1   Block 2

13 Add blue/purple bands between each row and at each end. Press all seams towards the bands. Piece should measure 24½ in x 26½ in.

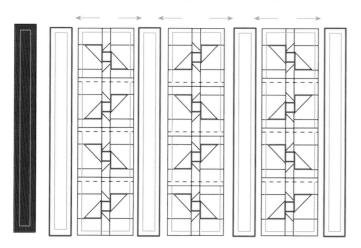

14 Layer fabric backing (26 in x 30 in leftover from 1¾ yd white tone on tone print fabric), batting, and pieced cushion top (see basting section, p9). Batting and backing will be larger than top, but will be trimmed after quilting.

15 Machine quilt all white areas (see machine quilting, p13) with a small loopy design.

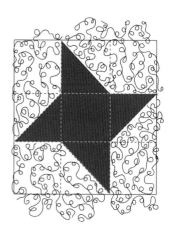

16 Trim all edges even with the cushion top.

17 Fold accent fabric strip in half lengthwise, wrong sides together, and press. Place pressed strips with raw edges even with the quilted cushion end. Sew through all layers with a scant ¼ in seam allowance. Press accent strips away from cushion top.

back of top
place the raw edges of the pressed accent fabric strip even with quilted cushion end & sew through all layers with ¼ in s.a.

18 Stitch the two long sides together to form a tube. Make sure that bands match and star points line up. Turn right side out.

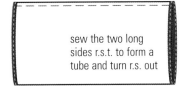

sew the two long sides r.s.t. to form a tube and turn r.s. out

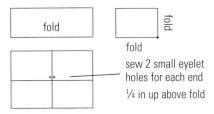

19 Bolster Ends Using the two 8½ x 24½ in pieces from step 3, fold each piece in half and fold a second time to find the center. Mark ¼ in from fold, as shown. Sew two small eyelet holes on these marks, sewing through one layer only. Repeat this step for the second end piece.

fold
fold
fold

sew 2 small eyelet holes for each end
¼ in up above fold

20 Bring the two short sides together and sew with ¼ in seam, right sides together. Turn right side out and refold on first fold. You have a tube with 2 raw edges and one fold.

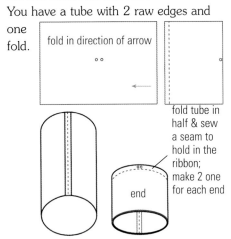

fold in direction of arrow

fold tube in half & sew a seam to hold in the ribbon; make 2 one for each end

end

21 Place the white end tube with eyelets facing the cushion top. Line up the raw edges and stitch with ¼ in seam allowance. Use great care as you sew through many thicknesses. Zig zag raw edge to prevent fraying.

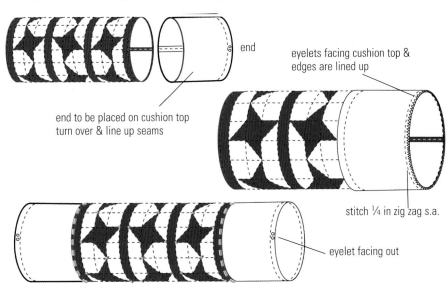

end

end to be placed on cushion top turn over & line up seams

eyelets facing cushion top & edges are lined up

stitch ¼ in zig zag s.a.

eyelet facing out

22 Using ribbon fabric and a bodkin, insert thread in first eyelet and come out at the second eyelet.

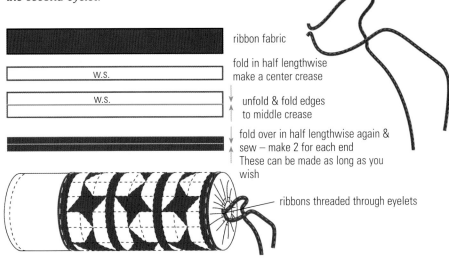

ribbon fabric

w.s.

w.s.

fold in half lengthwise make a center crease

unfold & fold edges to middle crease

fold over in half lengthwise again & sew – make 2 for each end
These can be made as long as you wish

ribbons threaded through eyelets

23 Add cut glass and seed beads at each star point of the bolster cover. Add a row of bugle beads along accent fabric strip.

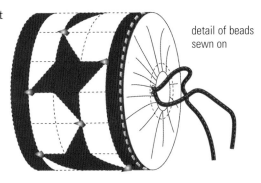

detail of beads sewn on

24 Cushion Sew the 24 in x
26 in white fabric in half (right sides
together) leaving about 4 in unstitched
for stuffing. Then sew two 8 in
diameter circles to the end of the
tube. Sewing with the circles on the
bottom makes it easier. Turn right side
out through the opening. Stuff with
poly fill and stitch opening closed.

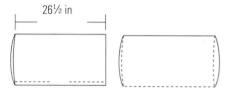

26½ in

Bolster Cushion Ends Pattern
half size

25 Insert cushion form into outer
cushion top.

❄️*Note* It is easier to pull the
cushion form from one end,
rather than push it in place.

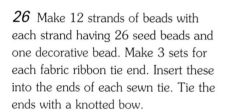

26 Make 12 strands of beads with
each strand having 26 seed beads and
one decorative bead. Make 3 sets for
each fabric ribbon tie end. Insert these
into the ends of each sewn tie. Tie the
ends with a knotted bow.

sew tassels into
ends of ribbons

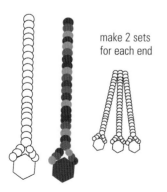

make 2 sets
for each end

finished bolster

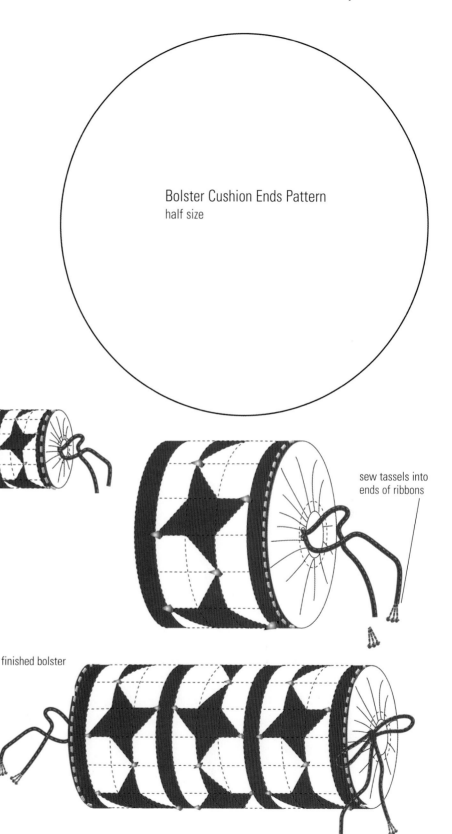

Friendship Stars Nightgown Keeper

Materials

- white tone or tone print fabric 1⅛ yd
- blue/purple fabric 1 yd
- bead tassel
  135 seed beads,
  5 larger decorative beads
- 12 seed beads

The seasonal nightgown keeper adds Victorian charm to the winter bedroom setting. It folds to a compact size and provides attractive storage. Finished size 15 in x 19½ in.

Directions

1 Unit A Small Star Squares from white fabric, cut 1 strip 2½ in x width of fabric and cut strip into eight 2½ in squares.

2 Small Star Points from white fabric, cut 1 strip 3 in x width of fabric and cut strip into four 3 in x 3 in squares.

3 Small Star Points from blue/purple fabric, cut 1 strip 3 in x width of fabric and cut strip into two 3 in x 3½ in squares.

4 Small Star Squares from blue/purple fabric from remainder of strip, cut two 2½ x 2½ in squares.

5 Unit B Large Star Points from white and blue/purple fabric, cut 1 strip 3½ in x width of fabric of each color and cut each strip into two 3½ in x 3½ in squares. Using remainder of strip for each color, cut four 3 in x 3 in squares for star squares.

❋ *Note* See bolster for star block instructions on pp 32, 33. Make 2 blocks 6½ in x 6½ in using the A units and 1 block 8 in x 8 in using the B units. The A block star point units are trimmed to measure 2½ in x 2½ in. The B block star point units are trimmed to measure 3 in x 3 in.

6 Front Section from white fabric, Unit A, cut 1 strip 6½ in x width of fabric and cut strip into two 6½ in x 9½ in pieces and for Unit B cut two 4¼ in x 8 in pieces.

9 Lining from the leftover tone on tone white fabric, cut 1 piece 20 in x 43½ in.

10 Outer case cut 1 piece blue/purple fabric 20 in x 28½ in.

11 To assemble the flap sew the two 9½ in x 6½ in white pieces to 6½ in x 6½ in star blocks, as shown.

Piecing Star Points

see bolster p32 for making the star points

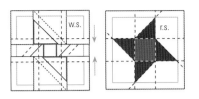

sew 4 white & 1 blue/purple squares to the 4 star point units. Press squares in direction of arrows

sew rows together & press in direction of arrows

Assembling the Flap

sew 6½ in x 6½ in star block to 6½ in x 9½ in white piece

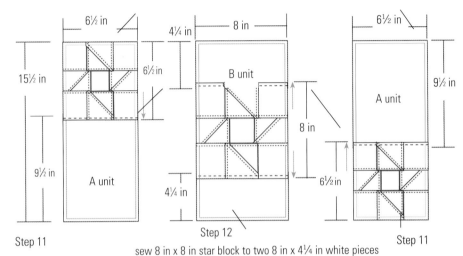

Step 11   Step 12   Step 11

sew 8 in x 8 in star block to two 8 in x 4¼ in white pieces

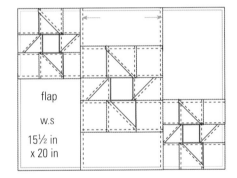

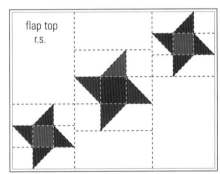

flap top r.s.

flap w.s 15½ in x 20 in

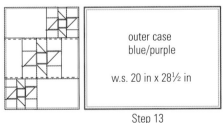

outer case blue/purple w.s. 20 in x 28½ in

bottom edge

lining w.s. 20 in x 43½ in

Step 13

Press seams to the white pieces (diagram step 11).

12 Sew the two 4¼ in x 8 in pieces to the 8 in star block.

13 Sew the 3 pieces together, making sure the seams match corners.

press in direction of arrows

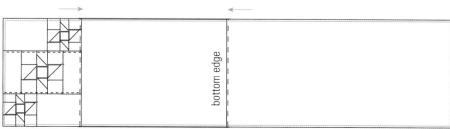

entire pieced unit is 20 in x 86½ in

bottom edge

step 15

fold in half w.s.t.

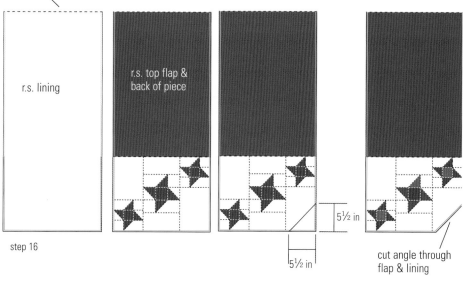

r.s. lining

r.s. top flap & back of piece

5½ in

5½ in

cut angle through flap & lining

step 16

fold   fold

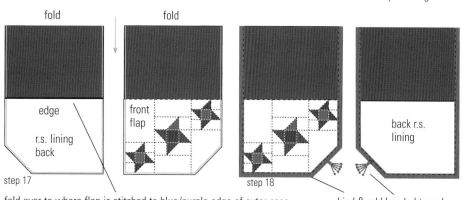

edge

r.s. lining back

front flap

back r.s. lining

step 17

step 18

fold over to where flap is stitched to blue/purple edge of outer case

bind & add beaded tassel

14 Press seams towards side pieces. *Note* Pieced flap unit should measure 20 in x 15½ in including seam allowance.

15 To assemble the keeper sew flap to the 20 in x 28½ in blue/purple piece and press seam toward blue/purple piece. Sew the 20 in x 43½ in lining piece to the bottom edge of the blue/purple piece. This entire unit should measure 20 in x 86½ in.

16 Fold in half, wrong sides together, along last stitched seam with the top and lining even along side edges. Measure 5½ in up the right side and across the bottom edge. Cut away this triangle through the top flap and lining.

17 Fold the bottom edge up to where flap is stitched to the blue/purple outer case, as shown. *Note* This forms the pocket for the nightgown.

18 Bind all raw edges (see p13 for general directions).

19 Add seed beads to star points.

20 To make a beaded tassel, make 5 sets of stranded beads and one decorative bead per strand. Join strands together by wrapping a strand of perle cotton around the tops, securing strands with some stitches.

Attach the beaded tassel to the middle of the cut angle of the flap using matching thread.

front flap

finished nightgown keeper with flap folded down in front

Patchwork Heart
Toss Cushion

This winter heart pillow shows off all your fancy needlework and is a delightful accent to room decor. Heart measures approximately 12 in x 16 in includes lace.

Stitches cretan, blanket, chevron, fly, straight woven, feather, stem, lazy daisy, chain, straight stitches couched in place, colonial & French knots

Materials
- foundation piece 12 in x 15 in
- cotton pieces in cream and taupe
- backing 12 in x 16 in
- poly stuffing
- embroidery threads
- beads
- Cluny lace 3¼ yds

Scrappy Patch Method

1   start with one 5 sided scrap material piece in the center of foundation fabric and sew in place

2   lay 2nd scrap on top r.s.t. of sewn 1st patch, and sew ¼ in s.a. along one side

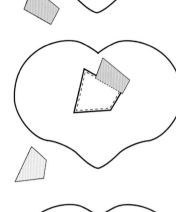

3   press 2nd scrap away from center

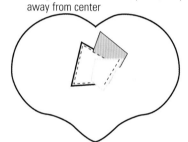

4   lay 3rd scrap on top r.s.t. clockwise to sewn 2nd patch and sew ¼ in s.a. along one side. Press 3rd patch/scrap away from center

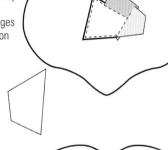

5   press 3rd scrap outwards towards edges of foundation piece

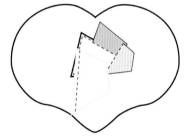

6   lay 4th scrap on top r.s.t. clockwise to sewn 3rd patch and sew ¼ in s.a. along one side

7   sometimes a seam cannot be stitched & is tucked under s.a. and secured on top with embroidery stitches

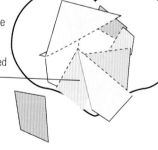

8   finished scrappy patchwork is ready for template pattern to be laid on top & cut

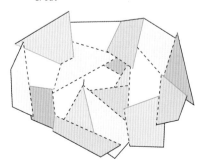

9   piece is ready to be embroidered

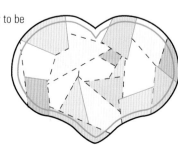

Directions

1   Cover the foundation fabric with patchwork pieces, as shown.

2   Make template (p8) for heart shape (p41) and place on patchwork. Cut out.

3   Embroider the pieced top using these stitches: stem, back, blanket, pistil, herringbone, feather, cretan, lazy daisy chain, satin, closed blanket. Branch is stem stitch filled in with chain stitches, berries are colonial & French knots, snowflakes are straight stitches couched in the center with fly stitches and French knots.

4   Place embroidered heart on top of backing, right sides together. On sewing machine, sew around edge with ¼ in seam allowance. Leave 3 in unstitched.

5   Turn right side out and press edges lightly to create a sharper edge.

6   Carefully stuff cushion with small pieces of poly fill, keeping the top and backing smooth and lump free.

7   Turn in opening edges ¼ in and stitch with small stitches using matching thread.

8   With thread matching Cluny lace, tie a knot in the bottom of thread and take a stitch ½ in from where you

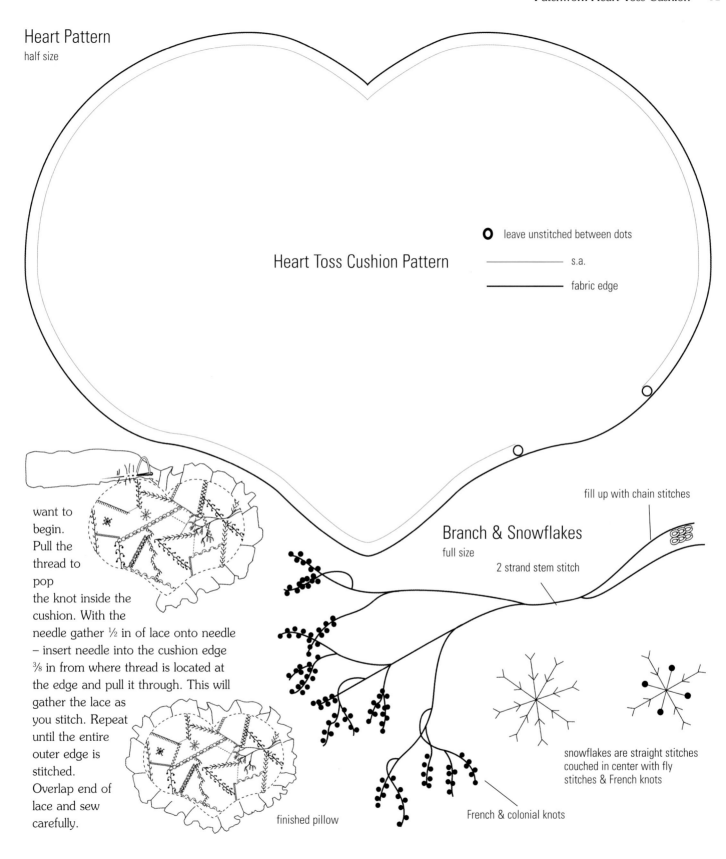

Heart Pattern
half size

Heart Toss Cushion Pattern

O leave unstitched between dots

s.a.

fabric edge

fill up with chain stitches

Branch & Snowflakes
full size

2 strand stem stitch

want to
begin.
Pull the
thread to
pop
the knot inside the
cushion. With the
needle gather ½ in of lace onto needle
– insert needle into the cushion edge
⅜ in from where thread is located at
the edge and pull it through. This will
gather the lace as
you stitch. Repeat
until the entire
outer edge is
stitched.
Overlap end of
lace and sew
carefully.

finished pillow

French & colonial knots

snowflakes are straight stitches
couched in center with fly
stitches & French knots

Crazy Patch Greeting Card

Materials

- handmade paper cards (any size)
- matching envelopes
- quilting scraps
- embroidery thread
- seed beads

Purchase handmade paper cards from your local craft shop or stationery store and use the leftover pieces from quilting projects to make unique personal greeting cards for every occasion.

Directions

1 Use a piece of flannel fabric as the base and cut it slightly larger than the opening you wish to make (see template patterns on this page). For this card I used a 3 in circle opening.

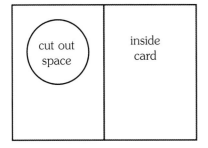

2 Assemble pieces of fabric of different shapes to cover the base fabric and machine stitch or hand sew pieces together and to base. See p44 for detailed instructions. Press.

3 Embroider a tree branch on the pieced winter scene with stem stitch, French knots, or add seed beads.

4 Place the trimmed embroidered piece over the hole inside the card and glue a piece of paper over back to give the inside a smooth look.

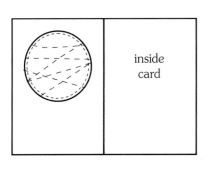

Patterns templates for holes
half size

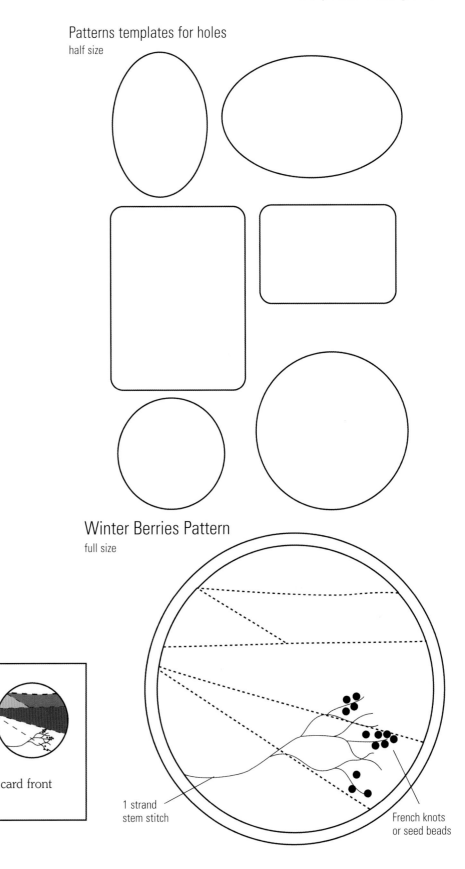

Winter Berries Pattern
full size

1 strand
stem stitch

French knots
or seed beads

Card Fabric Assembly

This uses the same method as the scrappy patch method on p40 except the scraps are progressively layered downward

1   start with one fabric scrap (r.s.facing up) on top of the foundation fabric covering the upper section & place a 2nd piece r.s.t. with the 1st fabric scrap

2   sew a seam across the top 2nd fabric scrap with ¼ in s.a.

3   press open

5   repeat with remaining fabric scraps until the foundation fabric is completely covered with the desired fabrics

4   sew a 3rd scrap r.s.t. with the 2nd scrap at a different angle & sew with ¼ in s.a.

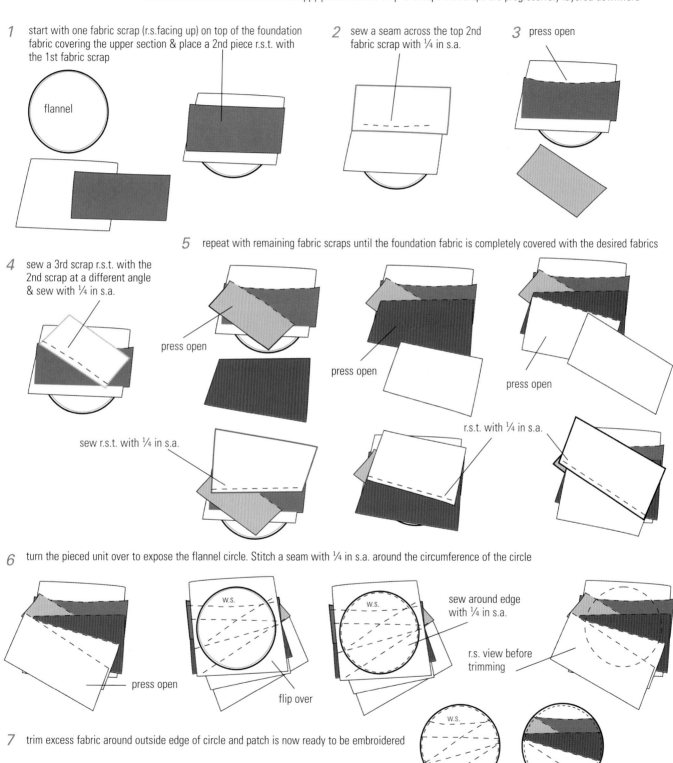

flannel

press open

press open

press open

sew r.s.t. with ¼ in s.a.

r.s.t. with ¼ in s.a.

6   turn the pieced unit over to expose the flannel circle. Stitch a seam with ¼ in s.a. around the circumference of the circle

w.s.

w.s.

sew around edge with ¼ in s.a.

r.s. view before trimming

press open

flip over

7   trim excess fabric around outside edge of circle and patch is now ready to be embroidered

w.s.

Spring

Strawberry Time
Banner

Materials

- background sky fabric approximately 25 in x 25 in
- frame 4 bias cut brown strips 1 in x 28 in
- red fabric 14 in x 28 in
- green 8 in x 12 in
- batting 3 pieces
  26 in x 26 in (banner)
  14 in x 14 in (strawberry)
  8 in x 8 in (leaves).
- Backing approximately 27 in x 27 in
- Binding 6 in x width of fabric
- Embroidery threads green and yellow

This seasonal banner introduces spring berries and fresh reds and greens. Finished size 24 in x 24 in quilted background with hanging sleeve and appliquéd berry.

Directions

1 Use freezer paper for strawberry and leaf templates, making 4 leaf templates.

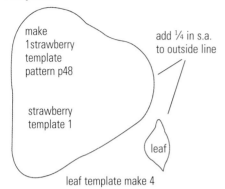

make 1strawberry template pattern p48

strawberry template 1

add ¼ in s.a. to outside line

leaf

leaf template make 4

 Note These templates are ⅛ size. You may use this as your guide or use the pattern on p48

2 Prepare background with frame (see p18).

3 Layer red fabric by folding in half, right side together. Iron number 1 strawberry template to wrong side of fabric. Place fabric layers on top of 14 in x 14 in batting piece. Using matching red thread, sew around the entire outer edge of strawberry shape.

r.s. fabric

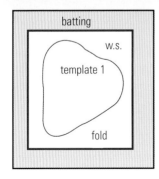

batting

w.s.

template 1

fold

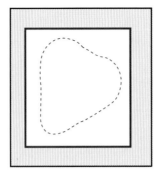

4 Trim around shape approximately ⅛ in beyond stitching line. Clip on the inside curve. Make a slit on the top layer of fabric only.

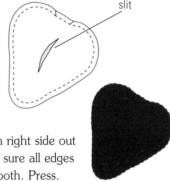

slit

5 Turn right side out making sure all edges are smooth. Press.

6 Prepare strawberry leaves pieces in the same way as the strawberry (steps 3 – 5) using the green fabric, green thread, and the 8 in x 8 in piece of batting.

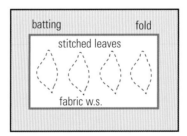

batting   fold

stitched leaves

fabric w.s.

⅛ in s.a. after trimming

slit

leaves turned r.s. out

7 Place on background. Prepare frame as on p18. Appliqué strawberry, slit side down.

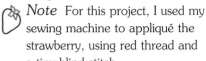 *Note* For this project, I used my sewing machine to appliqué the strawberry, using red thread and a tiny blind stitch.

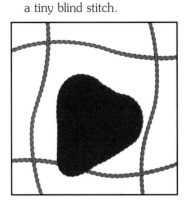

8 Place prepared leaves on top of the appliqué strawberry. Pin-baste in place with slit side down.

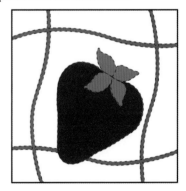

9 Using green thread and free-motion sewing machine foot, stitch veins, beginning with the bottom edge of each leaf.

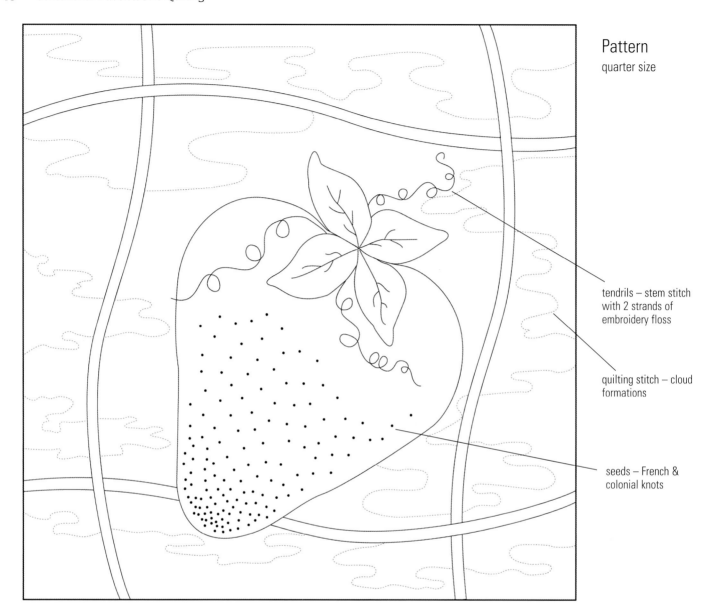

Pattern
quarter size

tendrils – stem stitch with 2 strands of embroidery floss

quilting stitch – cloud formations

seeds – French & colonial knots

use a stem stitch to embroider some tendrils & French or colonial knots for the seeds

quilt stitch cloud formations in the background & outline the strawberry & leaves

10 Using 2 strands green embroidery floss, embroider some curly tendrils with a stem stitch. Using 2 strands yellow floss make French and colonial knots (p16) to form the seeds of the strawberry.

11 Layer quilt background and baste. Suggested quilting: cloud formations in the background and outline quilting around the strawberry and leaves.

12 Add a hanging sleeve (p15).

13 Cut binding strips 2 in wide. See binding (p13). Sign and date the banner.

Strawberry Fields
Quilt

Materials

- background white tone on tone print 1¼ yds
- color 1 darkest red ¼ yd
- color 2 medium red mottled ¾ yd
- color 3 medium light red ½ yd
  & binding ¾ yd (1¼ yds total)
- color 4 green ½ yd
- backing 2¾ yds.
- batting 49 in x 49 in

This seasonal quilt features the double wedding ring quilt pattern which suggests delightful strawberry fields to carry out the spring motif. Finished size 46 in x 46 in.

Make freezer paper pattern (p8) or use template plastic (p8). Template includes ¼ in seam allowance.

Directions

1 Background uses units C (cut 32) & D (cut 12)

2 Fold fabric in half lengthwise. Mark and cut units using illustration as your guide.

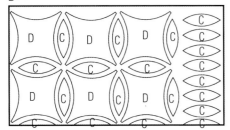

Some Cs are placed on the fold of fabric.

3 Place all units on fabric close together to save fabric. Grain line can be lengthwise or crosswise. Cutting through two layers will speed up the cutting process.

4 Color 1 (darkest red) Fold fabric in half lengthwise. Using Unit A mark and cut 8.

Color 2 (medium red-mottled) Fold fabric in half lengthwise. Using Unit A mark and cut 32.

Color 3 (medium light red) Fold fabric in half lengthwise. Using Unit A mark and cut 24.

Color 4 (green) Mark and cut fabric using Unit B. Cut 64.

Sewing the units

1 Sew Unit As to Unit Cs

Find the center of each unit by folding in half and creasing fabric in the seam allowance.

With A unit on top and C on bottom, right sides together and place pin in the center and at the end, as shown. Carefully stitch from V to V, making sure to line up the edges as you stitch (figure 1).

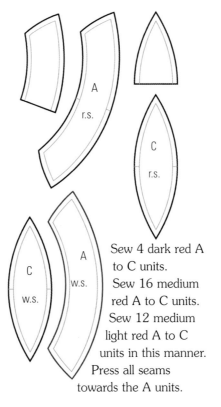

Sew 4 dark red A to C units.
Sew 16 medium red A to C units.
Sew 12 medium light red A to C units in this manner. Press all seams towards the A units.

Figure 1 Vs created by the placement of pieces

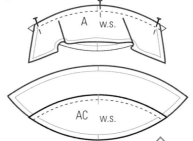

2 Sew Unit Bs to Unit As by sewing one B to both ends of all remaining A units.

Note There is a slight curve to this seam so stitch carefully. Press all seam allowances towards the As.

3 Sew pieced Unit A/B from step 2 to A/C units from step 1. Find the center point of each unit and crease lightly. Match up the center and pin. Place pins where the inside section

of As meet. With the A/C unit on the bottom, sew from end to end, lining up the edges as you stitch. Press seams towards A.

4 Sew pieced A/B/C units to Ds.

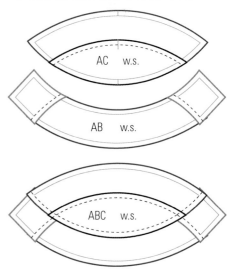

There are a total of 12 rings sewn into rows. Follow color code on p52. Begin and end with a backstitch. Sew the appropriate pieced unit to D with the D unit on the bottom. Match centers, pin, and stitch only from the top of the A unit to the end of A. Do not stitch into the B unit. Press all seam allowances towards the As.

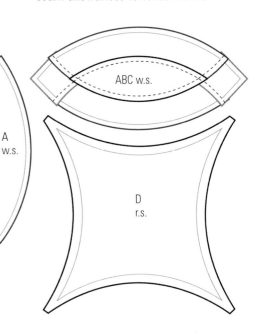

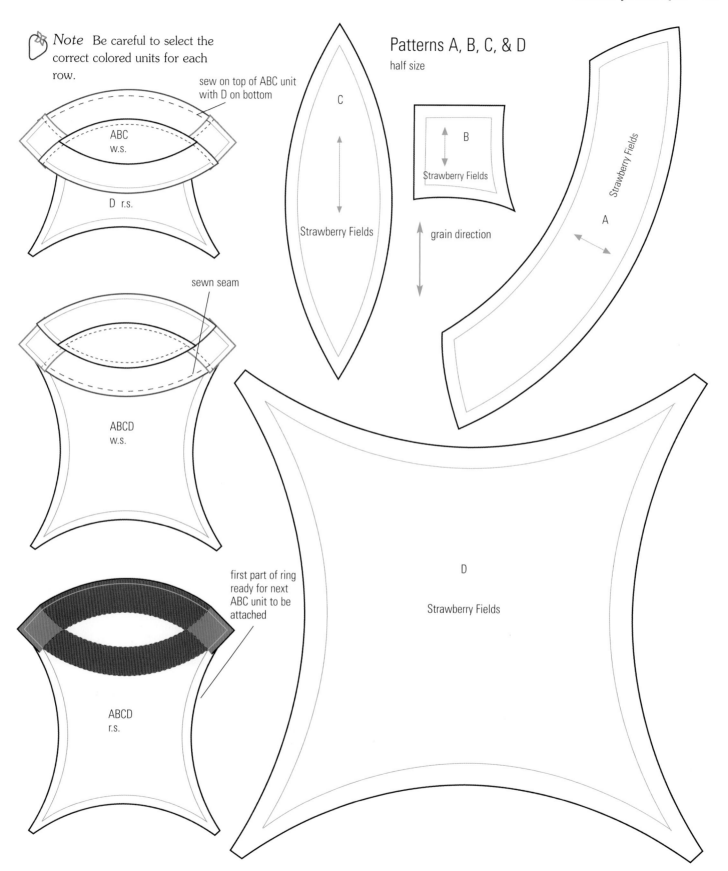

Note Be careful to select the correct colored units for each row.

sew on top of ABC unit with D on bottom

ABC w.s.

D r.s.

Patterns A, B, C, & D
half size

C

Strawberry Fields

B

Strawberry Fields

grain direction

Strawberry Fields

A

sewn seam

ABCD w.s.

first part of ring ready for next ABC unit to be attached

ABCD r.s.

D

Strawberry Fields

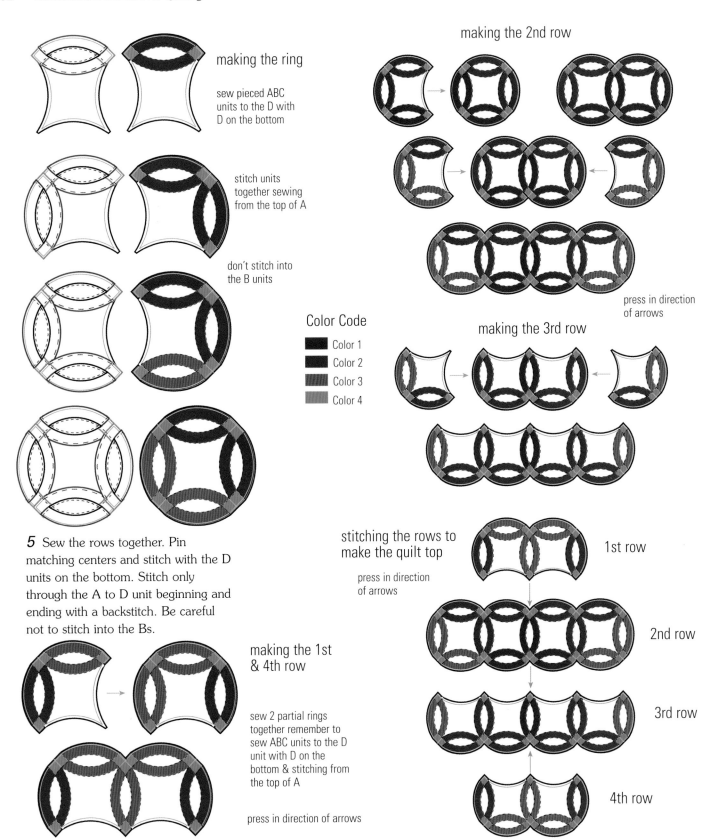

making the ring

sew pieced ABC units to the D with D on the bottom

stitch units together sewing from the top of A

don't stitch into the B units

Color Code

Color 1
Color 2
Color 3
Color 4

making the 2nd row

press in direction of arrows

making the 3rd row

press in direction of arrows

5 Sew the rows together. Pin matching centers and stitch with the D units on the bottom. Stitch only through the A to D unit beginning and ending with a backstitch. Be careful not to stitch into the Bs.

making the 1st & 4th row

sew 2 partial rings together remember to sew ABC units to the D unit with D on the bottom & stitching from the top of A

press in direction of arrows

stitching the rows to make the quilt top

press in direction of arrows

1st row

2nd row

3rd row

4th row

quilt top

detail of short seam stitched

6 Sew the Bs. The last seams to be stitched are the Bs. Place B units right sides together and stitch, beginning and ending with a backstitch. Press these short seams in opposite directions. Next stitch the cross seam to complete the B units. Press.

w.s. view

detail of cross seam stitched

stitch Bs together starting with short seams

place rings r.s.t. & stitch cross seam

completed stitching of Bs

w.s.

Pattern leaf veins in Bs
half size

example of quilting stitches

7 Cut backing in half crosswise. Remove selvage and stitch. Backing will be $49\frac{1}{2}$ in x approximately 83 in (This is larger than is needed).

8 Baste the quilt. Quilting suggestion: in D spaces quilt a strawberry and fill in with small squiggles. In the A sections quilt a wavy line approximately $\frac{1}{2}$ in from seams. In B sections (leaves), quilt veins.

quilt top with Bs stitched together

9 To bind from fabric color 3, cut five 2 in wide bias strips (see Binding p6).

finished quilt with binding sewn in

Strawberry Tea Cloth

This tea cloth is perfect for spring teas and patio suppers. The bright colors remind of flowers and green leaves. Finished size approximately 16 in diameter. Make several more for place settings.

Materials
- leftover fabric from the Strawberry Fields quilt.
- backing fabric 17 in x 17 in
- green embroidery floss
- red seed beads
- red embroidery floss

Directions

1 Follow the color chart and steps for the quilt instructions (p52).Cut 8 red Unit A.

2 Cut 8 color 4s (green) Unit B. Cut 1 background (white) Unit D. Cut 4 background (white) Unit C.

3 Following the sewing instructions for Strawberry Fields, piece one ring from steps 1 to 4 on pp50-52. Layer pieced ring with backing fabric putting right side together. With ¼ in seam allowance sew around outer edge leaving about 4 in unstitched.

completed ring w.s. ready to have backing sewn on

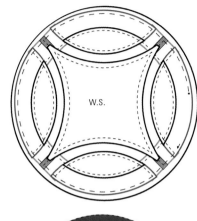

w.s.

backing r.s.

w.s.

sew backing & ring r.s.t. with ¼ in s.a. around the circumference leaving a 4 in gap

4 Trim backing even with edge of pieced ring. Turn right side out and stitch opening closed.

w.s.

r.s.

5 Using 2 strands green embroidery floss, embroider tendrils with stem stitch and add a few red beads along side of each tendril. Using 2 strands red floss, embroider outer edge with blanket stitch (p16) and add red seed beads to the top of each stitch.

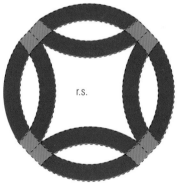

embroider veins for the leaves

sew red seed beads onto top of each blanket stitch

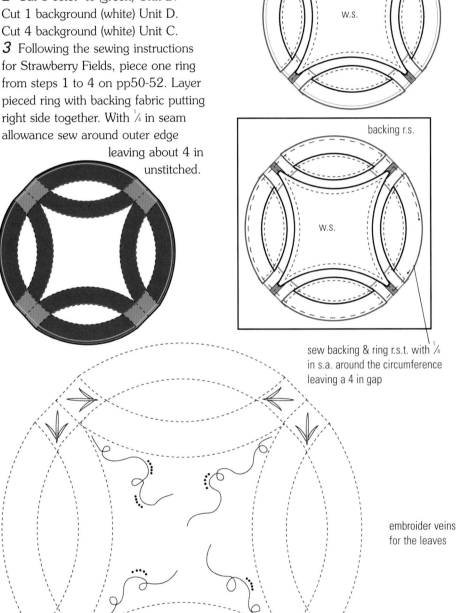

Strawberry Tea
Cozy Cover

T his colorful tea cozy cover carries on the spring motif and keeps the teapot warm even for outdoor dining.

Materials

- foundation or lining 2 pieces 16 in x 12 in
- batting 2 pieces 16 in x 12 in and 4 pieces $2\frac{1}{2}$ in x 4 in for leaves
- light blue fabric $\frac{1}{4}$ yd
- (A/B) dark red fabric (color 1) $\frac{1}{8}$ yd
- (C/D) medium red fabric (color 2) $\frac{1}{8}$ yd
- (E/F) medium mottled fabric (color 3) $\frac{1}{8}$ yd ($\frac{1}{16}$ yd would be enough for both colors 3&4 but I prefer extra)
- (G/H) medium red (color 4) $\frac{1}{8}$ yd
- (I/J) & binding light blue fabric $\frac{1}{4}$ yd
- leaves and top loops green fabric $\frac{1}{8}$ yd

Directions

1 Cut strips

Color 1 cut 3 strips $1\frac{1}{4}$ in x width of fabric

Color 2 cut 3 strips $1\frac{1}{4}$ in x width of fabric strips

Color 3 cut 2 strips $1\frac{1}{4}$ in x width of fabric strips

Color 4 cut 1 strip $1\frac{1}{4}$ in x width of fabric strips

Light blue cut 6 strips $1\frac{1}{4}$ in x width of fabric strips

making the 2 colored strips

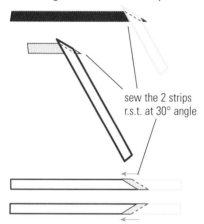

sew the 2 strips
r.s.t. at 30° angle

press in the direction of arrows

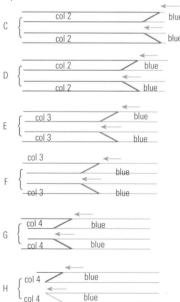

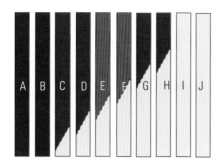

finished pairs of strips

2 Preparing base

Place foundation/lining fabric wrong side up and batting on top. With a pencil or marking tool that will show, find the center and draw a line, using a ruler (see below). Place pattern (p61) on top and trace around top edge, using center line as a guide. This will make it easier for placing strips later. Next, draw another line $\frac{1}{4}$ in to the right of 1st line. This is the placement line for the 1st strips. Repeat with the other foundation & batting piece.

lining w.s.

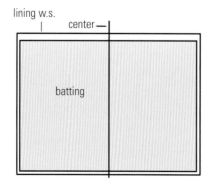

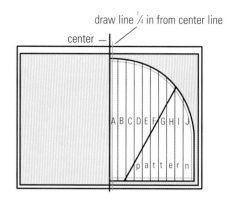

draw line $\frac{1}{4}$ in from center line

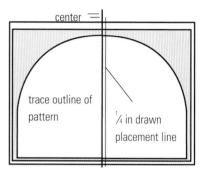

3 Sewing strips to base

Cut color 1 strips into 8 pieces $1\frac{1}{4}$ in x 12 in long (A/B).

Place 2 of these strips right side together and position with raw edge on the $\frac{1}{4}$ in from center line. Sew through all the layers with $\frac{1}{4}$ in seam allowance (you will be stitching through both layers of color 1, batting, and foundation). Open strip and press. Repeat with the other foundations, colors, and batting piece.

sew As r.s.t, with raw edge on placement line

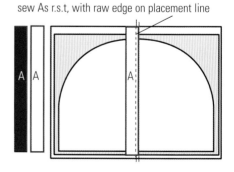

As pressed open & Bs ready to be placed

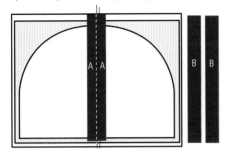

press open 2nd B & Cs ready to be placed

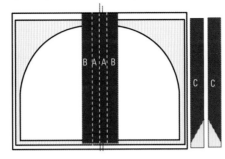

press open Cs & Ds ready to be placed

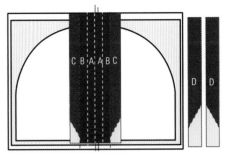

4 Add 2 more color 1 strips to each side of pieced center. Place right sides together with a ¼ in seam allowance and press. Repeat with other section.

sew 1st B r.s.t. with A with raw edges even

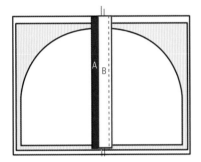

press open B & next B is to be placed

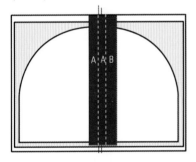

sew 2nd B r.s.t. with 2nd A with raw edges even

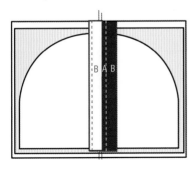

5 Make next set of strips C/D strips. Using color 2 cut 4 red pieces 1¼ in x 12 in and 4 red pieces 1¼ in x 10 in. Using light blue cut 4 pieces 1¼ in x 2½ in and 4 pieces 1¼ in x 4 in.
C Sew the 4 (color 2) 12 in pieces to the 4 blue 2½ in pieces at a 30° angle (you will find this angle on a ruler). Press seam towards the red.
D Sew the 4 (color 2) 10 in pieces to the 4 blue 4 in long pieces at a 30° angle, as shown p58.
Sew these onto batting/foundation by placing strip on top of B, raw edges even and r.s.t. Stitch through all layers with a ¼ in seam allowance Press.

 Note You will be adding the same C/D units to both sides of the center A/B strips. Make sure the 30° angles are facing the right way. Left and right sides are mirror images.

 Note Be sure to line up the seam where the red/blue meet so that the 30° angle continues to create the strawberry shape.

sew Cs r.s.t. with Bs with raw edges even

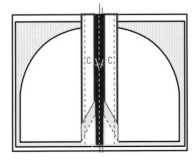

sew Ds r.s.t. with Cs with raw edges even

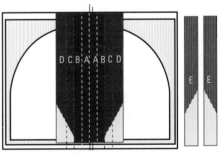

press open Ds & Es ready to be placed

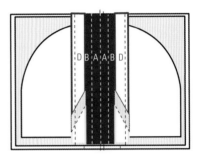

6 Make next set of E/F strips Using color 3, cut 4 red pieces 1¼ in x 8 in and cut 4 red pieces 1¼ in x 6¼ in. Using light blue, cut 4 pieces 1¼ in x 5½ in and 4 pieces 1¼ in x 7 in. Sew the 4 color 3 (8 in long red pieces) to the 4 pieces 5½ in long blue

press open Es & Fs ready to be placed

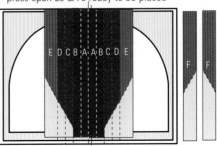

pieces at a 30° angle. This creates the E units.

Sew the 4 color 3 (6½ in long red pieces) to 4 blue 7 in long pieces at a

press open Fs & Gs ready to be placed

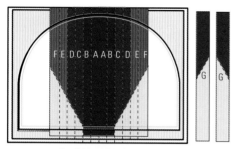

press open Gs & Hs ready to be placed

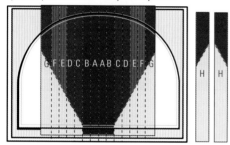

30° angle. This creates the F units. Stitch in place as in step 5.

7 Make next set of strips G/H. Using color 4, cut 4 red pieces 1¼ in x 4½ in long then cut 4 red pieces 1¼ in x 2½ in long. Using light blue cut 4 pieces 1¼ in x 8 in long then 4 pieces 1¼ in x 9½ in long.

Sew the 4 strips of color 4 (4¼ in long red pieces) to 4 blue 8 in long pieces at a 30° angle. This creates the G units.

Sew 4 strips of color 4 (2½ in long red pieces) to 4 blue 9½ in long pieces at a 30° angle. This creates the H units.

add blue I & J strips to complete the half cozy

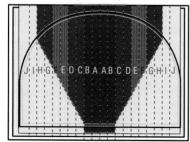

Stitch in place as in step 5.

8 Remaining sections are all blue I/J. Stitch in place.

Note Remember to repeat all steps for the other half, as well.

9 Strawberry leaves

Fold green fabric in half, right sides together. Trace 4 leaves onto the wrong side of green fabric. Place traced fabric on top of batting. Sew, using a small stitch, all around each leaf. Trim seam allowance to a scant ⅛ in and clip inside Vs. Make a slit in

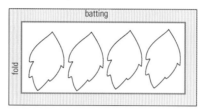
batting / fold

stitch leaves through all layers

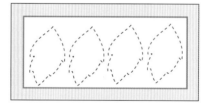

trim to ⅛ in s.a.　　slit in top layer　　back stitch veins

the top layer of fabric. Turn right side out and press. With green embroidery floss, backstitch veins on leaves.

10 Loop for top.

Cut one 1 in x 4½ in bias strip from green. Fold in half, wrong sides together. Stitch with ¼ in seam allowance. Turn right side out. Cut loop strip in half to create 2 small loops. Attach loop to top center of each tea cozy half, raw edges lining up with edge of tea cozy. Ends will be encased in binding later.

attach loop in center

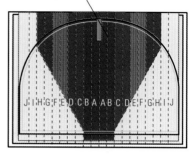

trim the 2 halves

place 2 halves lining to lining

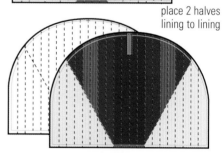

baste the 2 halves together

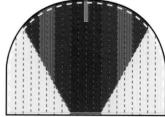

11 Trim edges of each half of tea cozy, as on pattern. Place lining to lining and baste the 2 pieces together.

12 Prepare binding

You will need about 68 in of 2 in pale blue bias for binding. Attach binding to top curved section, leaving the bottom edge open. Finish the binding to the back by hand and then bind the bottom edge.

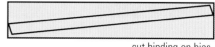

cut binding on bias

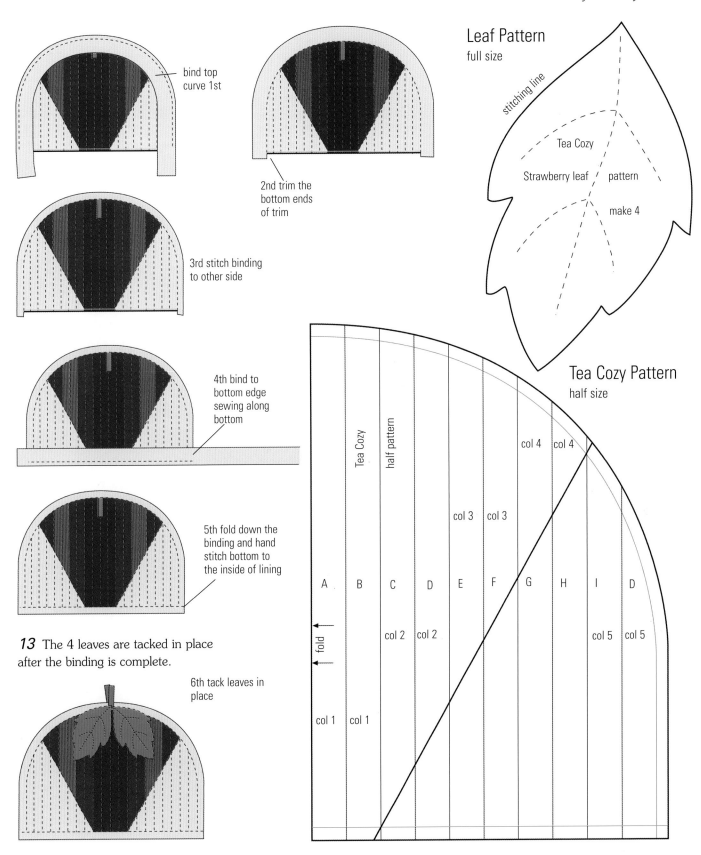

bind top curve 1st

2nd trim the bottom ends of trim

3rd stitch binding to other side

4th bind to bottom edge sewing along bottom

5th fold down the binding and hand stitch bottom to the inside of lining

13 The 4 leaves are tacked in place after the binding is complete.

6th tack leaves in place

Leaf Pattern
full size

stitching line

Tea Cozy

Strawberry leaf   pattern

make 4

Tea Cozy Pattern
half size

Tea Cozy

half pattern

col 4 col 4

col 3 col 3

A   B   C   D   E   F   G   H   I   D

fold

col 2 col 2

col 5 col 5

col 1 col 1

Strawberry Creamer Sugar Bowl Cover

Materials
- color 1 cut 8 in x 14 in (make extra 8 in x 8 in for backing)
- color 2 cut 8 in x 6 in
- green 2½ in x 5 in
- batting 2 in x 2 in
- green embroidery thread
- gold glass seed beads

This cover is perfect to protect sugar bowl or creamer for outdoor summer dining. Batting and beads make the cover heavy enough to stay in place. Finished size 7 in x 7 in.

Directions

1 Cut 2 pieces of color 1 and 2 using pattern (p64).

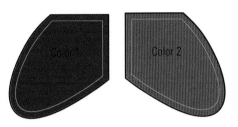

2 Sew 1 piece of color 1 and 2 together with ¼ in seam allowance (put color 2 on the bottom). Repeat with remaining units. Press seam allowance towards color 1.

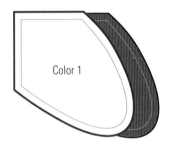

Color 1

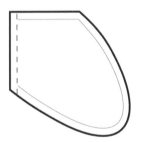

press in direction of arrows

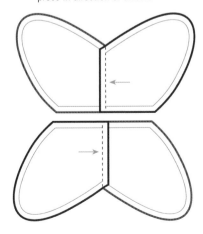

3 Sew pieced unit together, matching the center seam. Press.

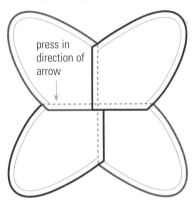

press in direction of arrow

4 Place backing and pieced top right sides together. Sew around outer edge with ½ in seam allowance. Leave approximately 2 in opening along one side. Trim seams to ¼ in and clip into Vs with sharp scissors. Turn right side out through opening. Press and hand stitch the opening.

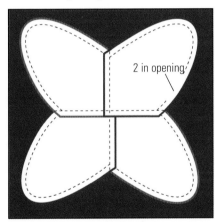

2 in opening

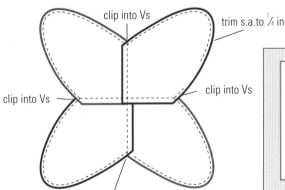

clip into Vs

clip into Vs

trim s.a.to ¼ in

clip into Vs

clip into Vs

clip into Vs

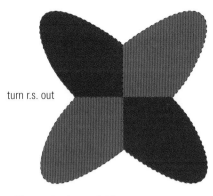

turn r.s. out

5 For leaf top fold green piece in half, right sides together. Trace leaf pattern onto the wrong side of fabric. Layer batting and marked fabric and stitch on traced line all around leaf shape.

trced pattern w.s. fabric

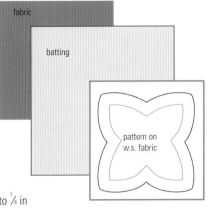

fabric

batting

pattern on w.s. fabric

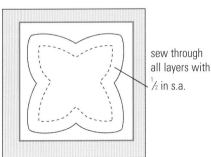

sew through all layers with ½ in s.a.

Strawberry Leaves Pattern
full size

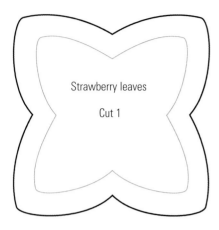

Strawberry leaves

Cut 1

6 Trim seam allowance and clip into Vs. Make a small slit in the top layer of fabric and turn right side out. Loosely stitch the opening with matching thread. Be careful not to stitch through the front.

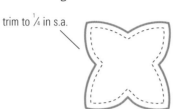

trim to $\frac{1}{4}$ in s.a.

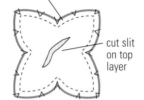

clip into Vs & outside curves

cut slit on top layer

Creamer/Sugar Bowl Cover Pattern
full size

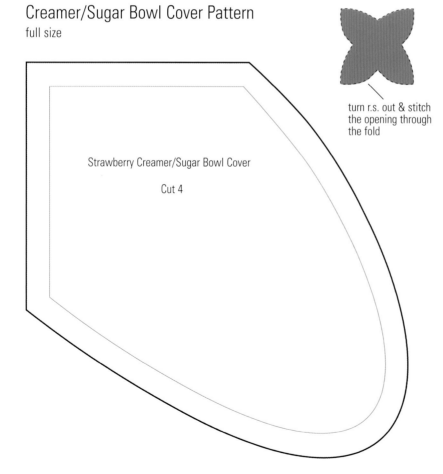

Strawberry Creamer/Sugar Bowl Cover

Cut 4

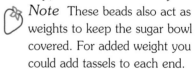

turn r.s. out & stitch the opening through the fold

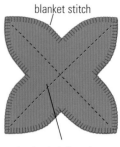

blanket stitch

7 With 2 strands of green embroidery floss, blanket stitch around the outer edge. Back stitch to create veins in the leaves.

back stitch for veins

8 Place leaf on top of cross seams of strawberry. Backstitch in place, forming a 4 leaf shape.

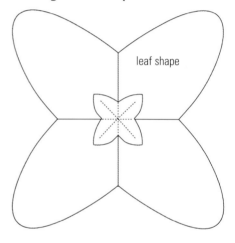

leaf shape

9 Add gold glass beads, concentrated at the tip, to look like strawberry seeds.

Note These beads also act as weights to keep the sugar bowl covered. For added weight you could add tassels to each end.

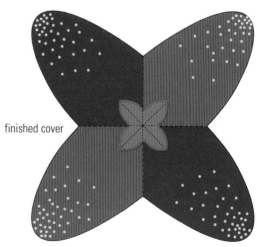

finished cover

Patchwork Heart
Toss Cushion

This spring heart pillow repeats the strawberry motif and shows off all your fancy needlework creating flowers and bugs. Finished size approximately 12 in x 16 in includes lace.

Materials

- foundation piece 12 in x 15 in
- cotton pieces in cream and taupe
- backing 12 in x 16 in
- poly stuffing
- embroidery threads
- iridescent thread
- beads
- cluny lace 3¼ yds

Tulip

flower outline with 2 strands stem stitch & fill in with chain stitch, cover with long & short satin stitches

straight stitches

stem use chain stitch

leaf top fill in with long & short satin stitches

leaf bottom fill in with satin stitch

Dragonfly

body fill with beads

wings outline with 2 strands stem stitch & fill in with satin stitch

legs use back stitch

head fill in with satin stitch

Strawberries

leaves fill in with satin stitch

tendrils outline using 1 strand stem stitch

fruit & stem outline with 2 strand stem stitch

leaves outline using tiny blanket stitch

blossoms outline with 2 strand lazy daisy stitch

outline bottom stem with 2 strand chain stitch

Snail

outline 2 strand stem stitch

fill in with satin stitch

strawberry fruit

1st - fill in with chain stitch

2nd - fill in with long & short satin stitches over top of chain stitches

3rd - embroider French knots for seeds

Stitches

Refer to embroidery diagrams p16 or choose your own stitches to cover the seams. Refer to the photo on p65 as a guide.

Directions

See Winter Heart Toss cushion p40 for patchwork technique. Use two strands of embroidery floss for your stitches except for the tendrils which use one strand.

Strawberries

fruit - outline with stem stitch, and fill in with chain stitches, then cover with long and short satin stitch and add seeds using French knots

leaves - outline with tiny blanket stitches and fill in with satin stitches

blossoms on strawberries lazy daisy stitch

stems - use stem and chain stitches

tendrils - use stem stitch with one strand embroidery floss

Snail

outline in stem stitch and fill in with satin stitch

Dragonfly

head - fill in with satin stitch

legs - back stitch

wings - outline in stem stitch and fill in with fly stitch using iridescent thread

body - fill in with beads

Tulip

flower petals - outline with stem stitch and fill in with chain stitches and cover with long & short satin stitches

For extra dimension go over the top of the bottom part of the petals with a few straight stitches with a green single strand of embroidery floss

leaf top - embroider a series of long and short satin stitches

leaf bottom - fill underside of the leaf with satin stitch

stem - fill in with tiny chain stitches

Crazy Patch
Greeting Card

Materials
- handmade paper cards (any size)
- matching envelopes
- quilting scraps
- embroidery thread

This lovely card will convey the warmth of your greeting and show a special friend how much you care.

Pattern
full size

blossoms
use French
knots

leaves
use 1 strand
lazy daisy stitch

stems
outline with 1 strand
stem stitch

strawberries
outline with 1 strand
stem stitch

strawberries
fill with satin
stitch

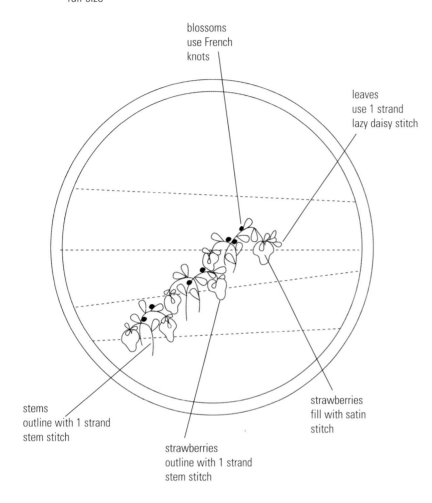

Directions

1 Cut out circle, p43. See instructions for piecing and assembly in Winter Crazy Patch Greeting Cards, p44.

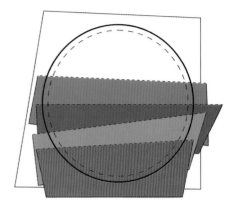

piece ready to be trimmed

2 Embroider with one strand embroidery floss.
strawberries – stem stitch outline of strawberries and fill in with satin stitches
stems – stem stitches
leaves - lazy daisy stitches
white blossoms – French knots

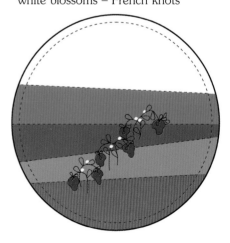

embroidered piece ready to be placed in card

Summer

Summer Sunflower Banner

Materials

- background summer sky fabric 25 in x 25 in
- frame 4 strips 1 in x 28 in bias cut brown
- yellow fabric ⅓ yd
- brown fabric ⅛ yd
- green stem and leaves ½ yd for stem cut on the bias, diagonal grain to allow for curves
- batting 26 in x 26 in plus 7 in x 8 in for leaves and 4 in x 9 in for center
- backing 27 in x 27 in
- binding 6 in x width of fabric
- beads brown glass that resembles seeds

This seasonal banner introduces the warm ripe shades of summer. The yellow sunflower is the theme. Finished size 24 in x 24 in.

Directions

1 Make templates using freezer paper from patterns below numbered 1 to 20. For stem (no template) cut one piece 1 in x approximately 31 in long on the bias (diagonal grain). If fabric piece is too small, cut 2 pieces and stitch together to create the required length.

make templates 1-20 patterns are quarter size

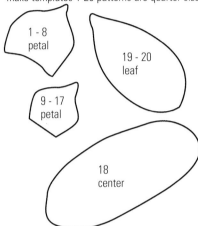

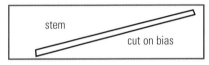

2 Prepare background.

3 Layer the yellow fabric by folding in half right sides together. Iron the templates (1-17) onto the wrong side of fabric leaving ¼ in space (seam allowance) around each shape.

4 With yellow matching thread and using small stitch on sewing machine,

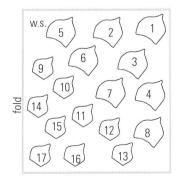

sew around outer edges of each piece leaving bottom edge open.

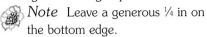 **Note** Leave a generous ¼ in on the bottom edge.

5 Trim other edges on all pieces close to the stitched line leaving ⅛ in seam allowance.

6 Clip into areas that have an inside curve. Turn each piece right side out. Be sure all seams are smooth. Press.

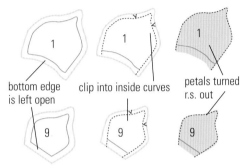

bottom edge is left open

clip into inside curves

petals turned r.s. out

7 Use remaining green fabric left over from cutting the stem. Place right sides together, iron templates 19 and 20 onto wrong side and trace around outer edge. Place fabric layers on top of batting. Remove paper template and stitch around entire outer edge of each leaf, making sure the batting is the bottom layer and using matching thread (green).

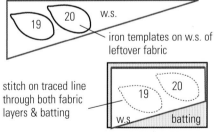

iron templates on w.s. of leftover fabric

stitch on traced line through both fabric layers & batting

8 Trim around each shape allowing ⅛ in beyond stitching line. Make a small slit through the top layer of fabric only. Turn right side out making sure all edges are smooth. Press. The slit side is the underside so you don't need to be concerned about the raw edge. I took the time to stitch it closed, but it could be left open.

trim to ⅛ in s.a. & make a small slit on top layer

turn r.s. out & sew slit closed if desired

9 Make the center using brown fabric and template 18. Follow steps 7 and 8.

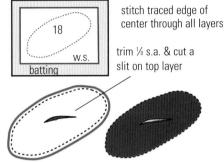

stitch traced edge of center through all layers

trim ⅛ s.a. & cut a slit on top layer

10 Press bias cut stem so seam allowance meets in the center. Stem will be a strip ½ in wide.

fold

fold

11 Place stem onto background (see appliqué, p10). I used my sewing machine and appliquéd the stem and sunflower center using a very tiny blind stitch with matching thread. First appliqué stem on both long sides (the ends will be covered).

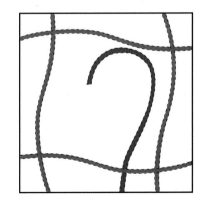

Pattern
quarter size

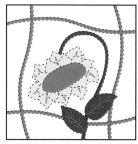

14 Place prepared center over raw edges of petals. Using matching thread blind stitch in place, making sure the slit is facing down.

15 Place leaves on top of stem, slit sides down. With matching thread and free motion foot, stitch veins starting right at the bottom edge and stopping approximately ¾ in from the tip and come back to the bottom.

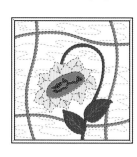

12 Position sunflower petals 1 to 8 so the extended bottom seam allowance is covered by the center. Pin baste petals in place. Using a variegated or yellow thread and motion foot on your sewing machine, stitch some veins on each petal.

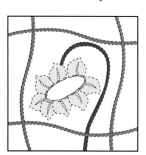

13 Position sunflower petals 9 to 17 overlapping where needed (see layout). Pin-baste in place and stitch around bottom (inside) edge making sure stitches are within the seam allowance. These stitches will be covered with the center. These petals are loose on the outer edges.

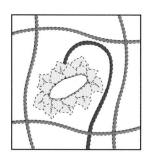

16 Layer and baste quilt
17 Add glass beads to the center to resemble seeds.
Suggested quilting cloud formation in the background.
18 Add a hanging sleeve (p15).
19 Bind (p13). Cut binding 2 in wide. Sign and date the banner.

Colors of Summer Quilt

Materials

- blue fabric 1¼ yds
- cobblestone fabric ¾ yd
- gray fabric ¾ yd
- green fabric 1 yd
- yellow fabric ½ yd
- brights (flower colors) fabric 32 – 3 in x 6 in pieces
- batting 1 piece 60 in x 75 in
- backing fabric 3½ yds
- binding 10 strips 2 in x width of fabric using 1 strip from 10 different flower colors or ⅝ yd of one color

This seasonal quilt introduces the full rich shades of summer used in an elegant pattern with uneven borders. Finished size approximately 55 in x 68 in. Make quilt larger by adding more squares.

Directions
Cutting Blue Units

Cut 8 strips 5 in x width of fabric then cross cut into 64 squares 5 in x 5 in and cut each square in half diagonally for a total of 128 triangles.

 Note Do not handle these triangles too much. The long side is bias and might stretch. If you spray fabric starch on fabric prior to cutting triangles fabric will be stabilized to minimize any stretching.

Cutting Cobblestone and Gray Units

Cut 9 strips 2½ in x width of fabric from each color. Cut 1 more strip 2½ in x width of fabric cobblestone only (needed in step 6 of Cobblestone Walk).

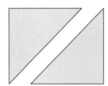

Cutting Green Units

Cut 10 strips 3 in x width of fabric and cross cut into 128 squares 3 in x 3 in then cut each square in half diagonally for a total of 256 triangles.

 Note Be careful not to stretch bias edge.

Cutting Yellow Units

Cut 5 strips 3 in x width of fabric and cross cut into 64 squares 3 in x 3 in.

Cutting Brights

Cut each 3 in x 6 in piece into 2 squares 3 in x 3 in (you will have two 3 in squares of 32 colors). Brights are flower colors.

Sewing Flower Garden Sections

1 Place 1 yellow and 1 bright color square right sides together. Draw a diagonal line on wrong side of yellow square. Repeat this step on all remaining yellow and bright squares. You will have 64 sets.

2 Sew a ¼ in seam on both sides of drawn line.
Note If you do not have a ¼ in pressure foot on your sewing machine, you may want to draw a stitching line.

3 Cut stitched unit on the drawn diagonal line. Press seams towards bright colors. Trim all pieced half square triangles to measure 2½ in x 2½ in. You will have 128 pieced flower units.

Note Only 110 will be used in the quilt – 12 units can be used for the table runner.

press toward arrows

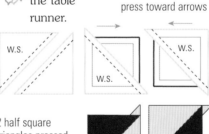

2 half square triangles pressed open ready for trimming

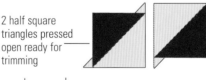

squares trimmed to 2½ in square

4 To each of the pieced flower units add 1 green triangle. Position the green unit on top, right sides together, with the right edges lined up, as

shown. The long side of green triangles are on the bias so handle with care. Press seam allowance to green. Repeat with remaining flower units.

sew green triangles.r.s.t. on right side of flower unit

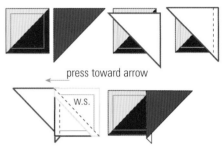

press toward arrow

5 To each pieced flower unit add second green to flower/green unit, as shown. Sewing onto pieced unit from step 4 on top line up bottom and left side. Press seam allowance towards the green. Repeat with all remaining flower units.

line up bottom & left sides – sew across bottom

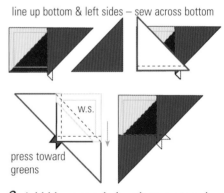

press toward greens

6 Add blue triangle by placing pieced flower unit and blue triangle right sides together. Both long edges are bias. Sew the 2 pieces together stitching as carefully as possible through the intersection.

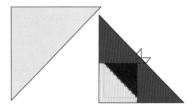

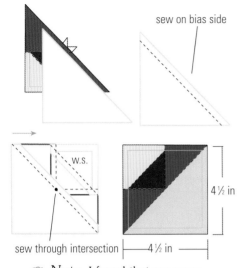

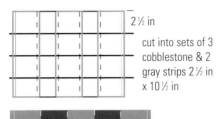

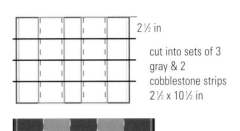

Note I found that my seam allowance was a little more than ¼ in. To achieve correct seam placement, trim seam allowance to ¼ in. This will eliminate the added bulk from the center.
Press seam allowance towards the flower unit. Trim block to 4½ in x 4½ in if needed.

Note Complete one unit. Check trimmed block. Adjust center seam to ensure your trimmed seam allowance is correct.

Sewing Cobblestone Walk
(be sure to use ¼ in seam allowance.)
1 Make 1 set for 3 cobblestone fabric pieces with 2½ in x width of fabric and two gray 2½ in x width of fabric.
Sew 1 cobblestone and 1 gray together. Press towards gray. Then add 1 cobblestone strip and press towards gray. Keep adding the appropriate strip, pressing each time, as shown (width of the strip must be 10½ in wide from edge to edge).

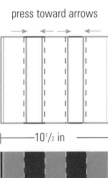
press toward arrows

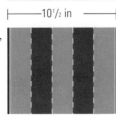

2 Cross cut pieced set into 2½ in pieces, keep pieced strip straight on the cutting board as you cut.

2½ in
cut into sets of 3 cobblestone & 2 gray strips 2½ in x 10½ in

Note It is easier to cut if wrong side is facing up. This helps to hold pieced unit tight against the board, eliminating slippage. From pieced fabric you will need 20 units 2½ in x 10½ in.

Note Depending on the width of the fabric you will get 16 units from the pieced set. The remaining 4 will be made later from leftover units from step 3 – 4 and be assembled in step 6.

3 Make 1 set 3 gray 2½ in x width of fabric and 2 cobblestone 2½ in x width of fabric. Sew strips together, pressing after each addition.

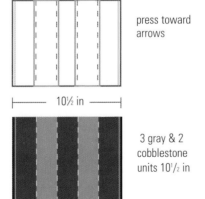
press toward arrows

10½ in

3 gray & 2 cobblestone units 10½ in

4 With the wrong side up, cross cut the pieced strip into 2½ in x 10½ in units. You will need 12 units 2½ in x 10½ in.

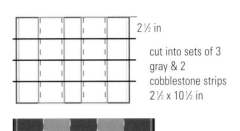
2½ in
cut into sets of 3 gray & 2 cobblestone strips 2½ x 10½ in

5 Sew remaining 4 cobblestone 2½ in x width of fabric and 4 gray 2½ in x width of fabric strips into 4 sets of 2, as shown. Width of pieced unit must be 4½ in. You will need 64 units 2½ in x 4½ in.

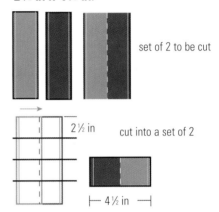
set of 2 to be cut

2½ in
cut into a set of 2

4½ in

6 Make remaining 4 units 2½ in x 10½ in from step 3 and 4. Remove one gray square from each unit.
Cut 4 squares 2½ in x 2½ in from the 2½ in x width of cobblestone.
Sew these squares to the ends of each unit. These are the remaining 4 units you will need for a total of 20 as in step 2.

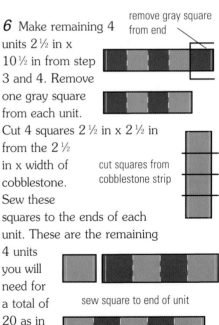
remove gray square from end

cut squares from cobblestone strip

sew square to end of unit

Assemble 4 Corner Blocks

1 Sew 2 blue triangles to both sides of step 5, Cobblestone Walk. Press seam towards cobblestone making a total of 4. Add second blue triangle to left side.

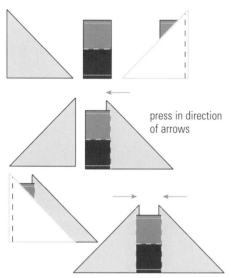

press in direction of arrows

2 Sew 2 flower garden sections to both sides of step 5, cobblestone making 4.

🌸 *Note* The flower sections will be of different colors.

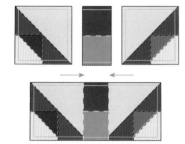

3 Sew the two units from steps 1 and 2 to both sides of Cobblestone Step 1. Press seam allowance towards cobblestone. You will have 4 corners.

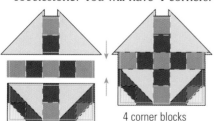

4 corner blocks

Assemble 10 Edge Side Block

1 Sew 1 blue triangle flower garden section to the sides of step 5, cobblestone. Press seams towards cobblestone making a total of 10.

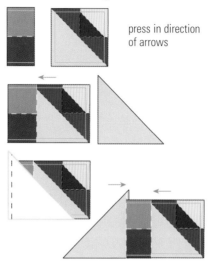

press in direction of arrows

2 Sew 2 flower garden sections to the sides of step 5 cobblestones. Press seams towards cobblestone.

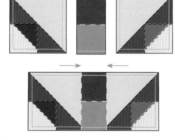

3 Sew the two units from steps 1 and 2 to both sides of cobblestone (steps 1 and 2 from Cobblestone Walk). Press seam allowance towards cobblestone. Make a total of 10 edge side blocks.

press in direction of arrows

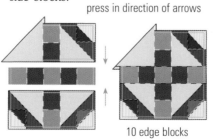
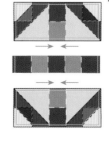

10 edge blocks

Assemble 18 Middle Blocks

1 Sew 2 flower garden sections to the sides of step 5, cobblestone. Press seam toward cobblestones. Make 6 blocks.

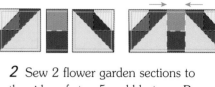

2 Sew 2 flower garden sections to the sides of step 5, cobblestone. Press seams towards cobblestones. Make 6 blocks.

press in direction of arrows

3 Sew the two units from steps 1 and 2 to both sides of cobblestone (steps 1 and 2 from Cobblestone Walk). Make 6 blocks.

press in direction of arrows

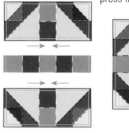
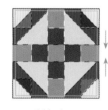

6 blocks

4 Repeat steps 1 and 2 using some cobblestone from step 5 by positioning the pieced unit section with dark gray on top/bottom. Press seams towards cobblestones.

5 Sew these pieced flower garden sections to cobblestone (steps 3 and 4 Cobblestone Walk). Make 12 blocks.

press in direction of arrows

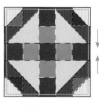

12 blocks

Assemble Quilt

Note Be sure to position blocks so that the cobblestones are alternating and the same flower/bright color appears in each corner.

1 Press blocks in each row in opposite directions.

Note All seams should match if pressing and stitching are done accurately.

simplified diagram

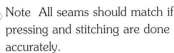

4 corners

10 edges

18 middle blocks total

6 middle – (3 cobblestone)/ (2 gray)

12 middle – (3 grays/ 2 cobblestones)

press in direction of arrows

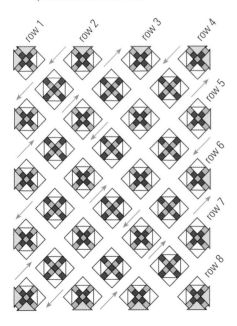

row 1 row 2 row 3 row 4 row 5 row 6 row 7 row 8

2 Sew rows together. Press seams in direction of arrows.

press in direction of arrows

quilting stitches
eighth size

flower

leaf

busy insects

3 Baste batting and backing to quilt top (see p 9 instructions).

4 Quilt (see above for suggestions. I stitched busy insects, leaf and flower images).

Binding

1 I used 10 bright flower colors for the binding. Cut 1 strip 2 in x width of fabric from 10 fabrics.

Sign and date your quilt

quilt top

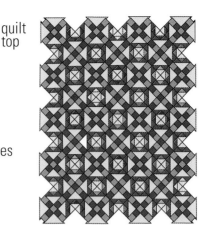

2 Cut each strip into 4 strips 2 in x 10 in. Layer the long sides together and cut them all at once to speed up the cutting time.

3 Sew these cut pieces together end to end at a 45° angle. Trim to ¼ in seam allowance. Press seam allowance open. Proceed as you would for Binding Quilt, (p13).

pieced binding with 10 bright flower colors

Colors of Summer
Table Runner

Materials

- 12 pieced flower units left over from Colors of Summer quilt
- cobblestone fabric 1¼ yd (used also for backing)
- binding create multi color binding from colors of fabric each 10 in x 2 in
- batting approximately 14 in x 45 in
- cut units using backing 14 in x 45 in
- cobblestone fabric 2 borders 5 and 6 2½ in x 32½ in
- 4 sashing strips 2½ in x 8½ in
- 1 square 9 in x 9 in cobblestone fabric cut in half diagonally to make 2 end triangles

This table runner uses the leftover pieces from the quilt coordinating the bright summer colors. Ideal for outdoor settings.

Directions

1 Sew pieced flower units following steps 1 to 6 in the Flower Garden Section of Quilt (p74). Piece 8 of these units into 4 sets of 2 and piece 4 of these into 1 block of 4 units.

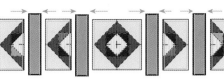

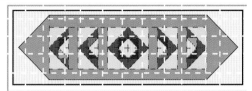

6 Layer with backing and batting. Baste. This table runner is quilted with the same images as the quilt.

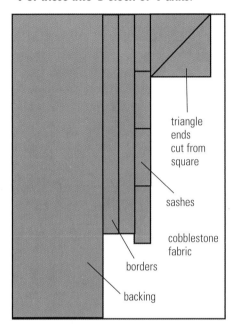

triangle ends cut from square

sashes

cobblestone fabric

borders

backing

sew pieced flower units

press towards arrows

3 Sew borders in place and press towards cobblestone border.

press towards arrows towards boarders

4 Sew triangles on each end making sure to center the triangle so the point is in the middle of the runner. The triangle is somewhat larger than needed but will be trimmed later.

7 Bind using multi colored pieces (see Binding Quilt (p77).

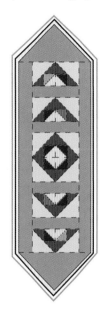

binding uses 10 strips of bright fabrics sewn together

4 blocks of 2 units

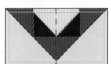

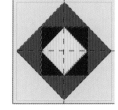

1 block of 4 units

2 Sew sashing to above units allowing ¼ in seam allowance. Press towards cobblestone sashing.

sew triangle ends & trim excess fabric

5 Press seams towards triangle. Trim extra fabric from the triangles using a square and rotary cutter.

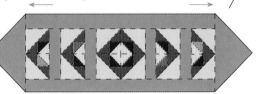

press towards arrows

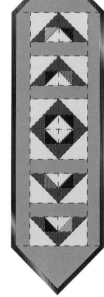

finished table runner

Colors of Summer Coasters

Materials

- 8 different brightly colored fabrics ¹⁄₁₆ yd of each
- backing fabric ⅛ yd
- binding fabric ⅛ yd
- batting flannel ⅛ yd

These coasters are made from the bright colors of summer fabrics. Make as many as you need for outdoor parties to add a splash of color to entertaining. Size 4 in x 4 in.

Directions

Cutting

Top

From each of the 8 fabrics, cut one 1 in x width of fabric strip and number each strip as example Color 1 yellow, Color 2 blue, Color 3 pink, etc.

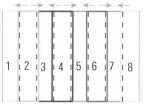

Backing

Cut one 4 in width of fabric strip. Cut strip into six 4 in x 4 in squares.

backing

Flannel

Cut one 4 in x width of fabric strip. Cut strip into six 4 in x 4 in squares.

flannel

Binding

Cut two 1¼ in x width of fabric.

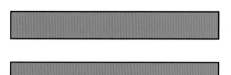

Assembling the coasters

1 Lay out the 8 fabric strips in a color pleasing manner.

2 Stitch together with ¼ in seam allowance. Sew pieced unit right sides together along the long side, joining color number 1 to color number 8, forming a tube.

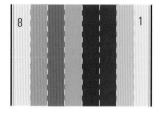

press in direction of arrows

stitch pieced unit r.s.t to make a tube

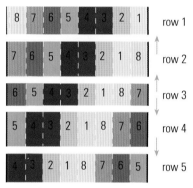

tube ready to be cut

3 Cut pieced tube into segments as follows per coaster,
cut two 1¼ in across
cut two 1½ in across
cut one 1 in across
Repeat same cuts for each coaster

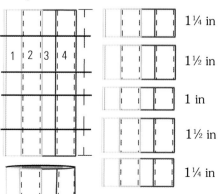

1¼ in

1½ in

1 in

1½ in

1¼ in

4 Unpick between numbers as illustrated in each row.
Row 1 unpick between 1 to 8
Row 2 unpick between 8 & 7
Row 3 unpick between 7 & 6
Row 4 unpick between 6 & 5
Row 5 unpick between 5 & 4
(This is suggested color sequence but by unpicking between different numbers a new design can be created.)
Some of the seams may have to be repressed so that all seams are opposite. This helps to match up the corners.

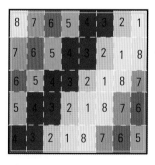

row 1
row 2
row 3
row 4
row 5

press in direction of arrows

5 Sew the rows together ¼ in seam allowance and press in the direction of the arrows. Press well! Should measure 4 in x 4 in.

stitched coaster top

6 Layer the coasters, backing wrong side up, flannel square, and coaster right side up. Line up all edges. Press all layers with hot iron to keep everything in place.

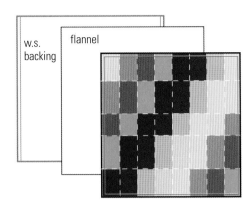

w.s. backing

flannel

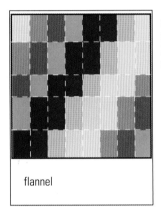

top, flannel, & backing layered, line up edges

flannel

 Note flannel shown longer for illustrative purposes only

7 Peel back half of the top of the coaster exposing the middle section as shown. Using sewing machine, sew along seam. This will quilt the layers together.

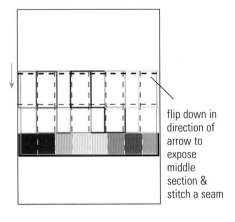

flip down in direction of arrow to expose middle section & stitch a seam

8 Peel back the other half exposing the other side of the middle section. With sewing machine, sew along that seam line. You will now have secured all 3 layers with a quilted line on each side of the middle section.

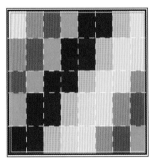

flip up in direction of arrow to expose middle section & stitch a seam

9 Press with hot iron and trim edges if needed.

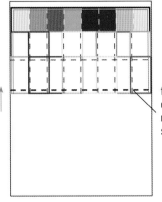

press & trim edges

10 Bind each coaster using the 1¼ in wide binding strips (see binding section p13).

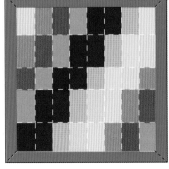

finished coaster

Note The colored unpick section in step 4 is just a guide. Try unpicking between different colors each time to create 6 different coasters.

Colors of Summer
Napkin Rings

Materials
- 11 different brightly colored fabrics each $\frac{1}{16}$ yd
- backing fabric
- buttons

These napkin rings match the summer coasters and brighten up a summer table. Use cloth or paper napkins in any color. Colored buttons add a festive touch.

Directions

Cutting

Outside

For each of the 11 fabrics, cut one 1 in x width of fabric strip. Number each strip, 1 yellow, 2 blue, etc.

Backing

Cut one 6 in x width of fabric strip.

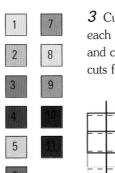

Assembling the napkin rings

1 Lay out the 11 different fabric strips in pleasing manner and stitch together allowing ¼ in seam allowance (sew 2 strips together press, add next strip, etc). Seams need to be pressed as illustrated below.

press in direction of arrows

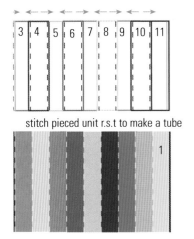

stitch pieced unit r.s.t to make a tube

2 Sew pieced unit together along the long side, joining color number 1 to color number 11, forming a tube.

tube ready to be cut

3 Cut pieced tube into segments. For each napkin ring cut 2 – 1¼ in across and cut 1 – 1 in across. Repeat same cuts for each napkin ring.

1¼ in   1 in   1¼ in

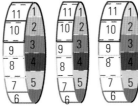

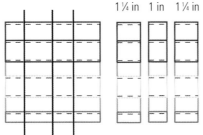

cut segments of tube ready to be picked between rows

1¼ in   1 in   1¼ in

4 Unpick between rows as shown.

Note By unpicking between different colors a new design can be created.

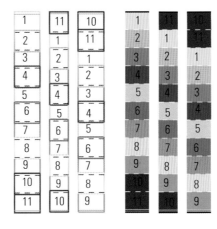

5 Sew the rows together allowing ¼ in seam allowance and press.

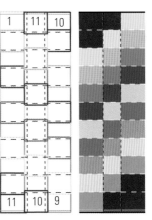

rows sewn together with ¼ in s.a.

6 Place pieced top and backing right sides together, lining up all edges. Sew around outer edge allowing ¼ in seam allowance, leaving approximately 2½ in open on one side. Turn right side out. Slipstitch opening closed.

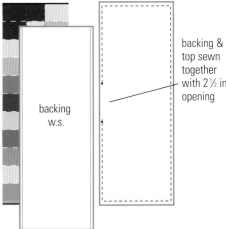

backing w.s.

backing & top sewn together with 2½ in opening

ends ready for buttons

7 Add buttons to the middle seams, joining the two ends together. Pull a napkin through the opening.

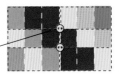

buttons sewn on joining the ends

finished napkin ring

Patchwork Heart Toss Cushion

This beautiful cushion picks up the sunflower motif and shows off all your fancy needlework. It makes a delightful accent to any room decor. The heart cushion is approximately 12 in x 16 in including lace.

Materials

- foundation piece
  12 in x 16 in
- cotton pieces in cream
  and taupe
- backing fabric 12 in x
  16 in
- poly stuffing
- embroidery threads
- Cluny lace 3¼ yds

Small Flower

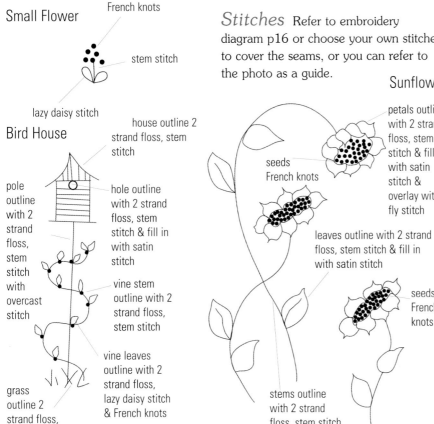

French knots

stem stitch

lazy daisy stitch

Bird House

house outline 2 strand floss, stem stitch

pole outline with 2 strand floss, stem stitch with overcast stitch

hole outline with 2 strand floss, stem stitch & fill in with satin stitch

vine stem outline with 2 strand floss, stem stitch

vine leaves outline with 2 strand floss, lazy daisy stitch & French knots

grass outline 2 strand floss, stem stitch

Stitches
Refer to embroidery diagram p16 or choose your own stitches to cover the seams, or you can refer to the photo as a guide.

Sunflowers

petals outline with 2 strand floss, stem stitch & fill in with satin stitch & overlay with fly stitch

seeds French knots

leaves outline with 2 strand floss, stem stitch & fill in with satin stitch

seeds French knots

stems outline with 2 strand floss, stem stitch

Directions

See Winter Heart Toss cushion p40 for patchwork technique. Use two strands of embroidery floss for your stitches.

Sunflowers

Stems – stem stitch

Leaves – stem stitch outline and fill in with satin stitch

Petals – outline with stem stitch with gold embroidery floss and fill in with satin stitch using same color embroidery floss, then overlay with gold metallic thread with fly stitch Center seeds – French knots

Bird House

House – outline with stem stitch

Hole – outline with stem stitch and fill in with satin stitch

Pole – stem stitch with overcast stitch Vine Stem – stem stitch

Vine Leaves – lazy daisy stitch and French knots

Grass – stem stitch

Small flower – French knots, stem stitch and lazy daisy stitch

Directions

1 Cut out rectangle. See instructions on p43 for piecing and assembly in Winter Crazy Patch Greeting Cards.

2 Stitch with one strand embroidery floss.

Flowers are embroidered with 2 layers of 2 shades of yellow lazy daisy stitches.

Leaves have green lazy daisy stitches. Flower centers are filled with brown French knots.

Sunflower stems are outlined with a green stem stitch.

Pattern three quarter size

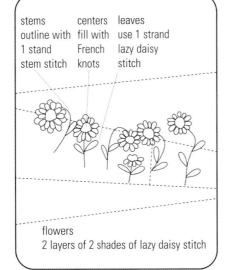

stems outline with 1 stand stem stitch

centers fill with French knots

leaves use 1 strand lazy daisy stitch

flowers 2 layers of 2 shades of lazy daisy stitch

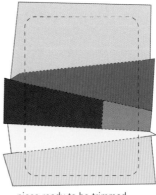

piece ready to be trimmed

embroidered piece ready to be placed in card

Crazy Patch Greeting Card

S end a personal greeting on a handmade paper card with your own sunflower motif embroidery to make it very special. See directions page 86.

Materials
- handmade paper cards (any size)
- matching envelopes
- quilting scraps
- embroidery thread

Autumn

Autumn Pumpkin Banner

Materials

- sky background blue 25 in x 25 in
- frame 4 bias cut brown strips 1 in x 28 in
- pumpkin 10 in x 15 in dark orange/rust fabric and 9 in x 9 in med.orange/rust fabric and 5 in x 9 in bright orange/yellow fabric
- stem 1½ in x 3½ in brown
  stem top 1½ in x 2 in taupe fabric
- leaves 8 in x 14 in dark green fabric
  leaf inset 4 in x 8 in mottled green fabric
- batting 26 in x 26 in
- backing 27 in x 27 in
- binding 6 in x width of fabric
- gold beads
- embroidery thread

This seasonal banner introduces the warm and vibrant shades of autumn as well as the produce that is associated with Thanksgiving pumpkin pies and Halloween lanterns. Finished size 24 in x 24 in.

Directions

1 Prepare templates (p8) using freezer paper. See pattern p93.

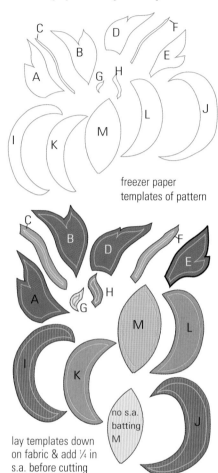

freezer paper
templates of pattern

lay templates down
on fabric & add ¼ in
s.a. before cutting

2 Appliqué brown frame in place (see p20 for placement instructions).

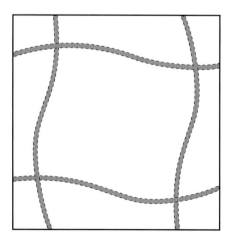

3 Prepare each leaf in 2 pieces. Appliqué the center line of first leaf onto C leaf inset. Appliqué the center line of second leaf onto F leaf inset.

Note It is easier to create the entire leaf and then appliqué to background. Follow these steps to create the leaves.

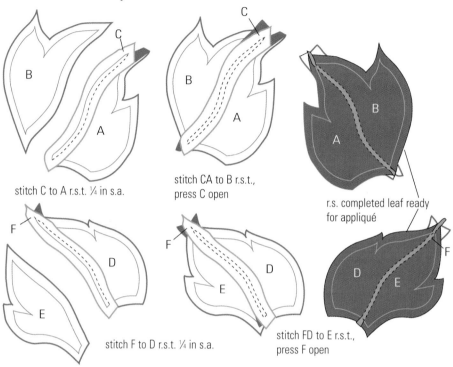

stitch C to A r.s.t. ¼ in s.a.

stitch CA to B r.s.t., press C open

r.s. completed leaf ready for appliqué

stitch F to D r.s.t. ¼ in s.a.

stitch FD to E r.s.t., press F open

4 Position and appliqué the 2 leaves in place, leaving bottom of each leaf unstitched (pumpkin will cover that area).

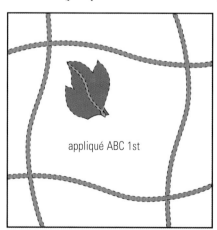

appliqué ABC 1st

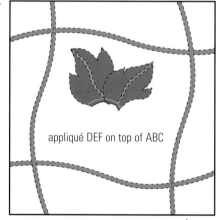

appliqué DEF on top of ABC

5 Appliqué stem top G to H before stitching to quilt top. Position and appliqué in place, paying special attention to the point at the top of G.

appliqué GH on top of leaf

7 Position K and L and stitch outside curves only.

K & L with s.a.

I   J

6 Position I and J (darkest pumpkin color). Stitch outside curves only.

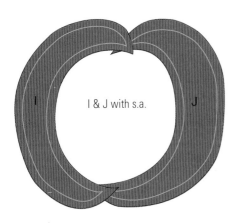

I   I & J with s.a.   J

9 Position M fabric over top of basted batting and appliqué in place.

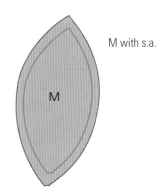

M with s.a.

M

8 Cut 1 piece of batting same size as template M. Baste in place. See step 11.

batting – no s.a.

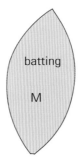

batting

M

10 Embroider pumpkin tendrils with dark gold thread using stem stitch. Sew gold beads along the bottom of K and L and M sections.

11 Layer quilt/baste quilt with backing and batting. See p8.

Pattern
quarter size

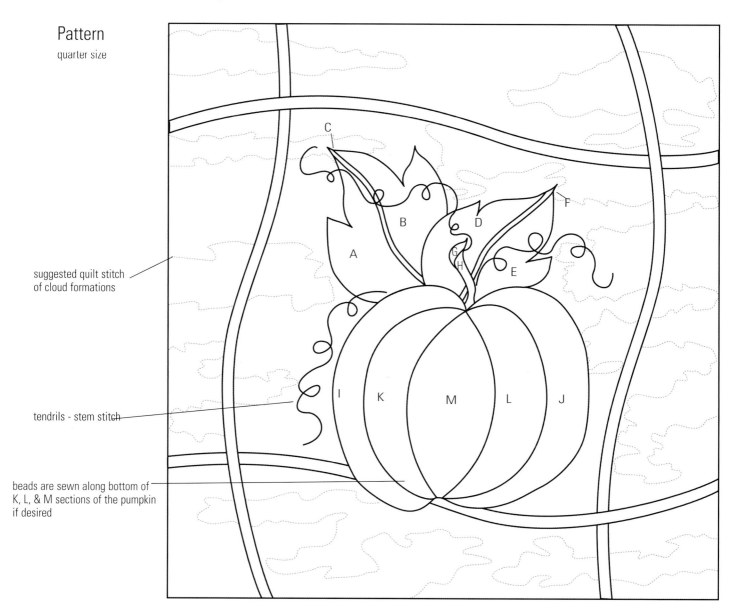

suggested quilt stitch
of cloud formations

tendrils - stem stitch

beads are sewn along bottom of
K, L, & M sections of the pumpkin
if desired

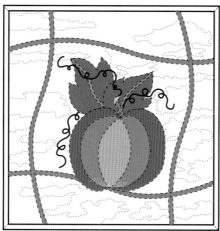

12 Machine quilt
stitch cloud
formations.
13 Bind (see p13).
Cut binding 2 in
wide.

finished banner with
quilt stitching &
binding

Harvest Stars
Quilt

Materials

- background black mottled fabric ⅞ yd
- various colors of fabric (greens, golds, rusts, red/orange, & brown, with total amount of fabric to measure 2 ½ yds
- binding black mottled fabric ½ yd
- batting 40 in x 46 in
- backing 42 in x 48 in

This small quilt is made from 42 blocks (6 across x 7 down) with an uneven border. Blocks measure 6 in x 6 in (including ¼ in seam allowance). Finished size of each block is 5 ½ in x 5 ½ in. Finished size of quilt is 39 in x 44 ½ in. Quilt can be made larger by adding blocks.

Directions

1 Make templates A & B (p8) from pattern (p100).

 Note Using spray starch on all fabrics helps keep fabric firm while marking and cutting, especially bias edges.

Making A

1 Using ⅞ yd piece of black mottled fabric cut 8 strips measuring 3¾ in x width of fabric.

2 Place 2 strips right sides together, lining up the sides.

3 Place template A on strip. Hold firmly and trace outline carefully with a white pencil or a marking pencil that will show. Flip template A, reposition at previous diagonal line and trace outline carefully. Repeat this procedure until you have 194 A pieces (168 for blocks, 26 for border).

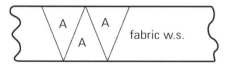

strips r.s.t. with template A outline traced

4 Cut out pieces using rotary cutter and ruler or a pair of sharp fabric scissors.

 Note If you use scissors pin the center of each piece to keep fabrics from shifting. Handle units carefully because bias edges can stretch and shift.

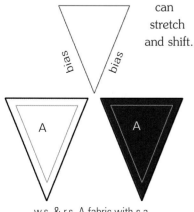

w.s. & r.s. A fabric with s.a.

Making B

1 Cut colored fabrics into 1¾ in strips along width of fabric. You will need 48 strips. Sort them into 12 sets (4 strips of different colors each).

 Note Don't spend too much time sorting. They all look great together in the end.

2 Place 2 strips right sides together and sew using an accurate ¼ in seam allowance. Press seam allowances in one direction.

3 Place remaining 2 strips from first set right sides together and sew, using an accurate ¼ in seam allowance. Press seam allowance in same direction as first 2 strips.

4 Sew the 2 stitched units together and press, creating a 4 strip unit.

 Note All seams should be pressed in the same direction.

5 Continue in this manner until all 12 sets are carefully sewn and pressed. Each pieced strip measures 5½ in deep x width of fabric.

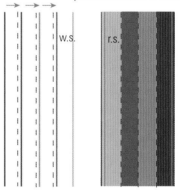

press in direction of arrows

strips stitched together with ¼ in s.a.

6 Place 2 pieced strip units right sides together (seam allowance will automatically nestle together because they will be in opposite directions).

7 Place template B on positioning line on the stitching line and mark with a sharp pencil, as shown.

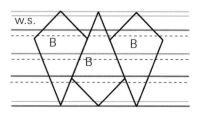

strips w.s. view – template B outline traced

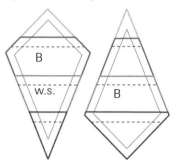

Bs cut from fabric strips w.s. view

8 Continue to make these units and carefully cut out 224. You will need 168 units for blocks and 56 for pieced border.

Bs ready to be sewn to As

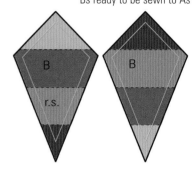

Piecing together the blocks

1 Sew blocks, carefully place one A piece and one B piece right sides together, with B on top. Sew ¼ in seam allowance starting at the top of piece and sewing down to the point, stopping ¼ in from the point. Backstitch a few stitches. Continue sewing these A and B pieces until you have 168 units.

 Note I like to "chain piece" these units. Take a few minutes to position the A and B pieces right sides together, then pick up the top two and sew.

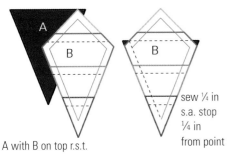

A with B on top r.s.t.

sew ¼ in s.a. stop ¼ in from point

2 Press each unit towards the black or A piece. Handle carefully, remembering not to stretch the bias edges.

press towards A

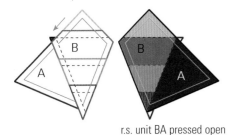

r.s. unit BA pressed open

3 To sew half blocks, place 2 pieced units right sides together.

Note The way the seams are pressed they will nestle together. Sew with A on top. Start at top and sew down to point, stopping ¼ in from point end (end with a few back stitches). You now have 84 half block units.

Note Press seam towards B.

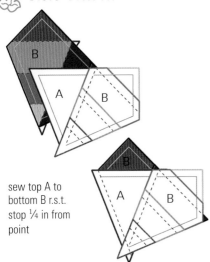

sew top A to bottom B r.s.t. stop ¼ in from point

5 To sew 2 half blocks together to create blocks, place 2 pieced halves right sides together (the seams in the center will nestle because they are pressed in opposite directions). Place a pin just below the center to keep unit from shifting.

press in direction of arrows

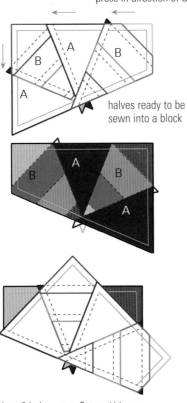

halves ready to be sewn into a block

place 2 halves r.s.t. & sew ¼ in s.a.

6 Starting at the edge of the block, sew from one edge to the center, remove pin, and continue to stitch to the end. Remember to start and stop with back stitches.

Note Be careful not to let the bottom layer at the center point shift as you sew. Use an awl or the point of the seam ripper to guide these layers right up to the pressure foot of the machine.

7 Sew one block first, then unfold the 2 halves and press all the seams in one direction. When properly pressed, the middle will fan out to create a star,

distributing the bulky center. Blocks measure 6 in x 6 in. You will need to make 42 blocks.

press in direction of arrows

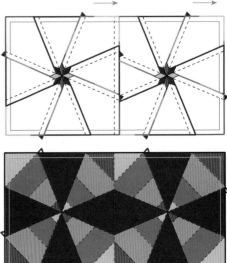

r.s. view of single block

8 Quilt center has 7 rows of 6 blocks. Sew blocks into rows, as illustrated, p96. Press seams carefully. Continue piecing rows together and pressing each row in the opposite direction.

diagram simplified

press in direction of arrows

Note When joining blocks, match up the seam allowances where A units meet. These seams are pressed so that they will nestle together. Use your seam ripper point to guide units while sewing so they won't move.

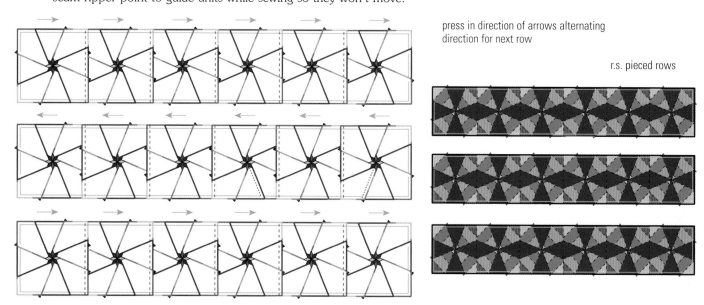

press in direction of arrows alternating direction for next row

r.s. pieced rows

9 Sew the rows together, watching that the seams remain in the direction that they are pressed. Join row 1 to 2, then add row 3, etc. Press all row seams down in one direction. The center of the quilt measures 33½ in x 39 in.

diagram simplified   press in direction of arrows

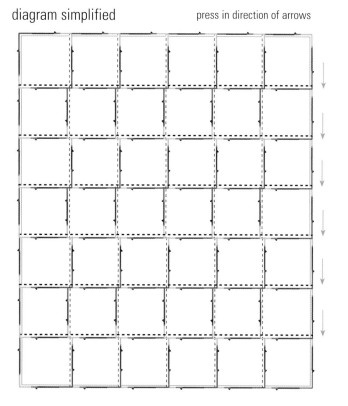

quilt top ready for borders

Piecing together borders

1 To create a pieced border, use the remaining A & B pieces.

2 Sew A and B into sets with A on top of B, right sides together starting with a backstitch at the top and end with a backstitch ¼ in from the point. Make 6 sets.

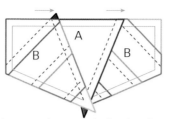

1 set w.s. view, press in direction of arrows

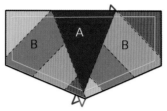

need 6 sets to make 1 border,

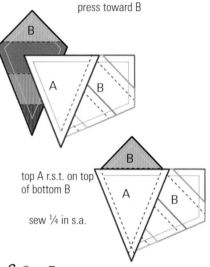

press toward B

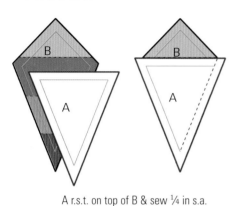

A r.s.t. on top of B & sew ¼ in s.a.

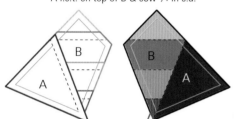

press toward B

3 Now add B piece to other side of A piece, as shown, and each time stop sewing ¼ in from the point.

4 Sew these 6 sets together, end to end, as shown. Press all in one direction. Make one more border like this (top and bottom borders).

press in direction of arrows

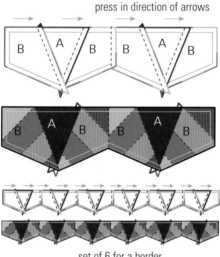

set of 6 for a border

5 To make side borders repeat steps 2 and 3. Use 7 A pieces and 16 B pieces per border.

top A r.s.t. on top of bottom B

sew ¼ in s.a.

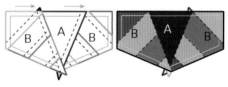

top A r.s.t. on top of bottom B

sew ¼ in s.a. stop ¼ in from point

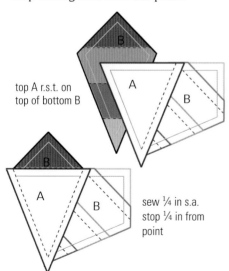

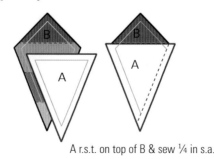

A r.s.t. on top of B & sew ¼ in s.a.

6 Sew 7 sets as in step 4. Now sew 7 sets together, end to end, as shown.

1 set, press in direction of arrows

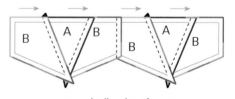

need 7 sets to make 1 side border

press in direction of arrows

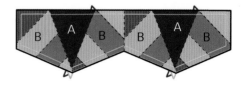

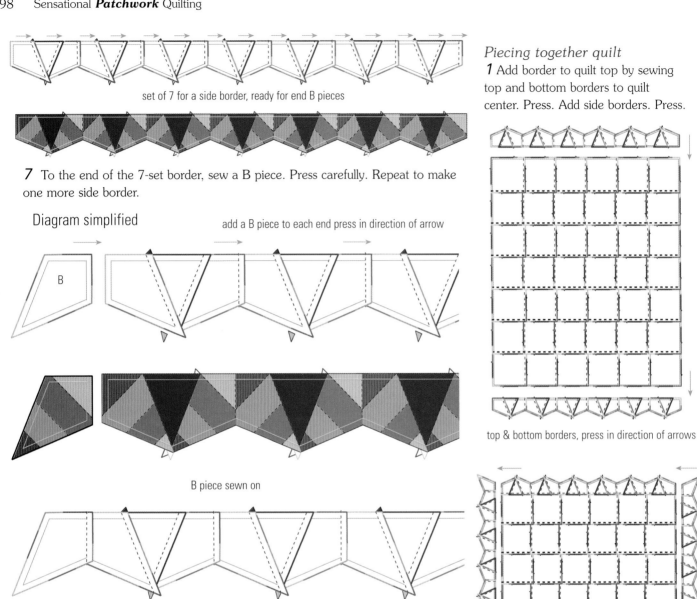

set of 7 for a side border, ready for end B pieces

7 To the end of the 7-set border, sew a B piece. Press carefully. Repeat to make one more side border.

Diagram simplified

add a B piece to each end press in direction of arrow

B

B piece sewn on

Piecing together quilt

1 Add border to quilt top by sewing top and bottom borders to quilt center. Press. Add side borders. Press.

top & bottom borders, press in direction of arrows

side borders, press in direction of arrows

2 Baste backing, batting, and the quilt. Quilting suggestion: Leaves see pp99-100.

3 To bind from black mottled fabric, cut nine 2 in wide bias strips (see Binding uneven edges p15).

w.s. quilt top showing pressed seams

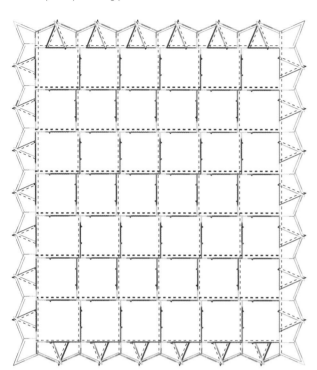

finished quilt with trim

r.s. view of quilt top ready for quilting

quilting stitches with suggested leaves to be stitched on the As,
& wavy line around edges of Bs

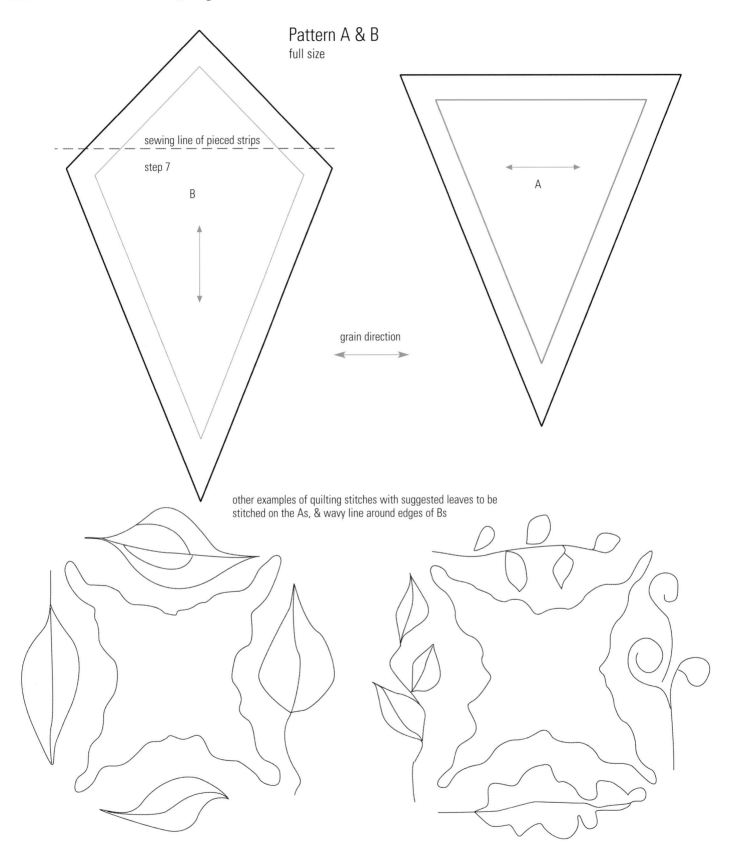

Pattern A & B
full size

sewing line of pieced strips

step 7

B

grain direction

A

other examples of quilting stitches with suggested leaves to be
stitched on the As, & wavy line around edges of Bs

Autumn Memories Pillow

Materials

- base piece muslin or plain cotton 27 in x 27 in
- cotton, silk, velvet pieces ¼ yd each in a variety of colors
- backing fabric 27 in x 27 in
- embroidery threads (6-stranded skeins, silk, perle cotton #8)
- over-dyed threads
- seed beads
- old lace
- 2 lbs poly stuffing or piece could be left flat and used as a table topper

This Victorian scrappy patch pillow with prairie points edge is made from a variety of fabrics in autumn colors, accented by colored embroidery threads and beads. Finished size of 26 in x 26 in includes prairie points.

Directions

1 Lay out base fabric square.
2 Cut out triangles, strips, diamonds, etc. from variety of fabrics.
3 Cut out a 5-sided center unit.
4 Place center unit onto the middle of the base fabric right side up.
5 With sewing machine, stitch just inside the cut edge to secure the center unit to keep it from shifting.

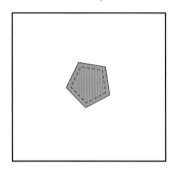

5-sided center piece stitched r.s. up to base

6 Place next piece, right sides together, on top of center unit. Line up edges and sew ¼ in seam allowance along side. Flip newly attached piece away from center and press. (See scrappy patch method p40).
7 Continue to add each piece in this manner until the base is covered.

 Note You may have to create some pieced units to cover awkward spaces. To do this sew a few cut pieces together, end to end, to create a large piece. With rotary cutter and ruler, recut a straight edge. This unit piece can then be added as if it were one piece.

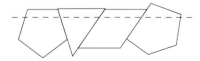

sew a few cut pieces end to end to create a large piece

8 To determine the outer edge of the covered base, measure and mark a square 24½ in x 24½ in which allows a ¼ in seam allowance to give finished size of 24 in square. With sewing machine stitch on marked line. This will secure the outer edge.

 Note Do not trim off excess at this time.

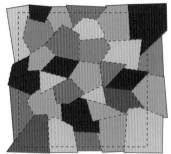

stitch on marked line 24 in sq

Hand Embroidery

Traditionally, each seam of crazy patchwork is covered with a line of embroidery. For this pillow I have chosen to place some embroidered images straddling some seams; therefore, I have left certain seams unstitched. The images are a weeping birch tree, sunflowers, ladybug, spider and web (traditionally a good luck symbol on crazy quilts), basket, cluster of grapes, fanciful tree, p104. Use 4 in embroidery hoop for this work.

Basket

1 Mark dot placements for top and bottom of basket.
2 Using perle cotton, place straight stitches from dot to dot, creating spine of basket.
3 Using second thread color, weave threads under and over the spine as follows. With knotted thread come up at A and weave under A and over and go down at B. See illustration for basket p104. Repeat with each horizontal row making sure to alternate the weaving threads through each spine.

4 To make bottom of basket and handle, use same thread color as the weaving thread and chain stitch basket handle plus one row across basket bottom edge.

 Note I also stitched a small series of straight stitches through the middle of each chain stitch of the basket handle using the spine color thread.

Cluster of Grapes

1 Make small pencil marks on pillow to place leaves. Outline leaves with stem stitch. Fill in with a satin stitch dividing each leaf in half and stitching in the direction shown.

 Note I used 3 strands variegated, over-dyed green embroidery floss.

2 Create the grapes using 3 colors with French & colonial knots.
3 Seed beads could be used for grapes instead of or as well as knots.

Ladybug

1 Outline with red stem stitch.
2 Fill in body with red satin stitch.
3 Use 2 small straight back stitches for legs with black thread.
4 Outline head with black stem stitch and fill with black satin stitch.
5 Make antennae with black stem stitch with a French knot at the end of each.

Fanciful Tree

1 Make branches with stem stitch.
2 Make leaves with lazy daisy stitch.
3 Make flowers using gold seed beads.

Weeping Birch Tree

1 Outline trunk and main branches using stem stitch.
2 Fill in tree trunk with chain stitch.
3 Make tree fronds using main green first, then stitch another layer of feather stitches with a lighter thread.

Sunflowers

1 Outline leaves with stem stitch. Divide leaves in half and fill in with satin stitch to look like veins of leaf.

2 Make sunflower stem using 2 rows of stem stitch.

3 Make vines using stem stitch.

4 Make vine leaves using stem stitch and fill with satin stitch.

5 Make ferns using fly stitch.

6 Make sunflower petals using stem stitch for outline and fill in with satin stitch.

7 Make sunflower center with 3 colors of brown French and colonial knots.

8 Sew gold seed beads to bottom of each leaf.

Spider and Web

1 Straight stitch main black lines with straight stitch.

2 Cross lines are woven with black thread.

3 Couch joints in place with a tiny straight black stitch.

4 Make spider body with bugle bead and head with a seed bead. Add small straight stitches with black thread for the legs.

5 All remaining seams are stitched with a variety of stitches, such as feather, cretan, herring bone, cross stitch, etc.

Finishing Edge of Pillow

1 When embroidery work is complete, check previous measurement to make sure it is 24½ in x 24½ in. Use leftover fabric pieces (cotton only) to make prairie points.

2 Cut out forty 3 in x 3 in squares and fold diagonally into quarters creating triangles.

3 Pre-stitch each of 4 borders by

fold in direction of arrows

placing triangles (as shown), overlapping edges so that ¼ in from each end measures 24 in.

4 Place pillow top right side up. Lay

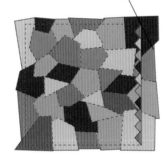

stitch where triangles meet   overlap triangles

one pre-stitched border on top, line up edge of border with marked line.

5 Baste with sewing machine close to edge.

1st stitched border

6 Position second border in the same way and baste. Repeat for two more borders.

diagram simplified

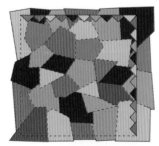

make sure all corners touch & meet square on

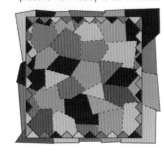

piece is now ready to be trimmed

7 The 2 corner triangles will touch each other. Trim base fabric to match edge of pre-stitched prairie points border. Then place top, right side down, onto backing and sew through all layers (¼ in seam allowance), leaving 6 in open for turning.

w.s. top

stitch trimmed base fabric on top r.s. down on backing

8 Trim backing fabric even with pillow top, making sure to bias cut the corners to eliminate bulk, as shown.

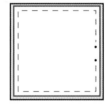

trim backing even with top & bias cut corners to eliminate bulk

9 Turn right side out through the opening and press.

10 To secure the layers stitch a few French knots at intersections.

Note This step will be used only if you leave piece flat as a table topper.

11 Stuff pillow with poly filling and close opening by hand with a small stitch.

12 Sign and date your work (p15).

finished pillow

Embroidery Patterns
full size

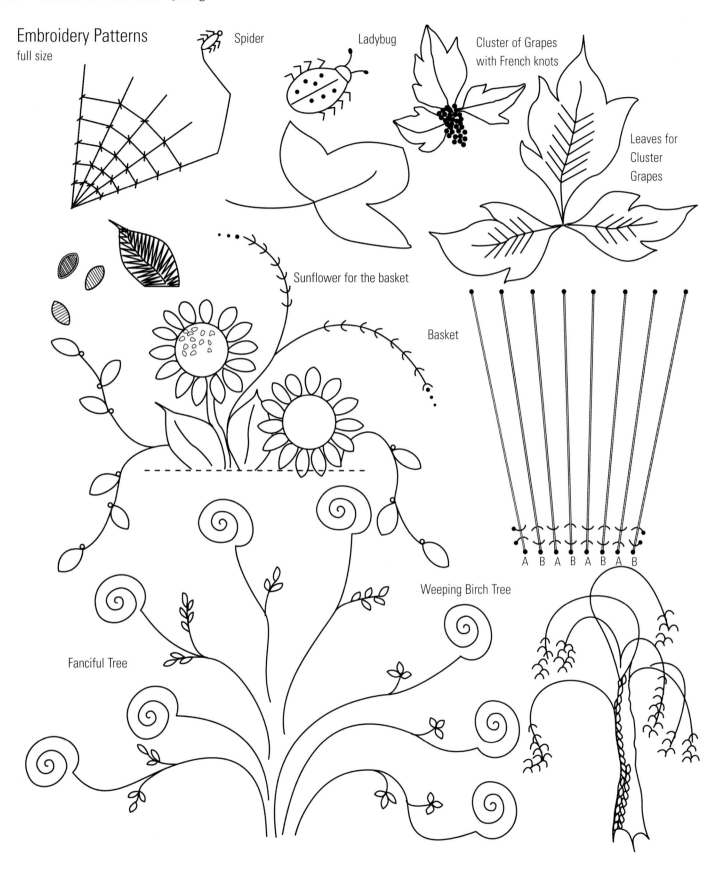

Spider

Ladybug

Cluster of Grapes
with French knots

Leaves for
Cluster
Grapes

Sunflower for the basket

Basket

A B A B A B A B

Weeping Birch Tree

Fanciful Tree

Stitcher's Companion Sewing Tote

Materials

- foundation 4 muslin pieces 10 in x 6 in
- A outside cover patchwork blue sky ¼ yd red/orange fabric ¼ yd light blue ⅛ yd (for B template and appliqué strip on cover orange fabric ¼ yd yellow/gold fabric ¼ yd scrap pieces of browns, greens, purples, and blues
- B inside lining light blue 11 in x 24 in
- cotton batting 11 in x 24 in and 1 piece 3 in x 9 in for needle case and pin cushion
- C pockets yellow/beige felted wool ½ yd of 36 in wide (18 in x 36 in)
- embroidery floss, various colors

This decorative tote holds all your favorite sewing tools. It can be hung on a wall or folded for travel. Dimensions are 9 ¼ in x 8 ¾ in (folded) and 9 ¼ in x 22 ¾ in (flat).

Directions

1 Create the outer tote using the scrappy patch method (p40). Cover the four foundation pieces as follows:

Panel F cover 10 in x 6 in piece with a variety of browns

Panel E cover 10 in x 6 in piece with browns and greens

Panel D cover 10 in x 6 in piece with greens and purples

Panel C cover remaining 10 in x 6 in piece with purples and blues

2 Trim all covered pieces to measure 9 ½ in x 5 in.

3 Sew all panels together with ¼ in seam allowance, as shown. Press seam allowance open to lessen bulk in seams. Pieced unit should measure 9 ½ in x 18½ in.

4 To create top of outer tote, trace pieced arc and pieced rays (p112)

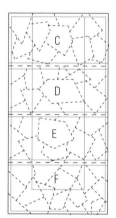

w.s. view of finished pieced cover, press seams open

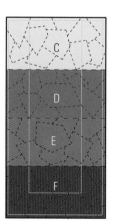

r.s. view of finished pieced cover

onto tissue paper (see paper piecing directions, p10). Use sky blue and red/orange for pieced arc, using the foundation paper piecing method.

Note All even numbered pieces are red/orange and odd numbered pieces are blue.

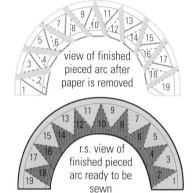

view of finished pieced arc after paper is removed

r.s. view of finished pieced arc ready to be sewn

5 Use orange and yellow/gold fabric to piece the pieced rays.

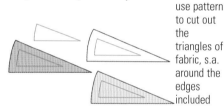

use pattern to cut out the triangles of fabric, s.a. around the edges included

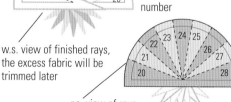

sew r.s.t. 20 & 21 triangles, repeat with 21 & 22, etc. until piece 28, press towards the smaller number

w.s. view of finished rays, the excess fabric will be trimmed later

r.s. view of rays

6 Make template for G and use to cut out from sky blue. Do the same for H from light blue.

G & H fabric w.s. cut out with s.a.

7 Sew G to the top of pieced arc, sew H to the inside of pieced arc. Sew H to the top of pieced rays.

Note The curve is quite extreme and requires careful pinning before stitching. You may find it easier to hand piece H to the pieced rays.

8 Cut 1 in x 40 in strip of light blue

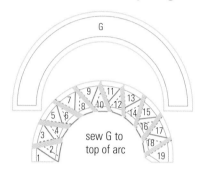

sew G to top of arc

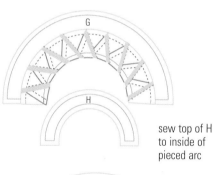

sew top of H to inside of pieced arc

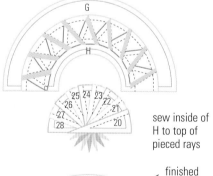

sew inside of H to top of pieced rays

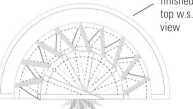

finished top w.s. view

trim exess point - even with bottom edge

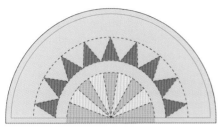

finished top r.s. view

fabric. Fold 2 side edges inward ¼ in, as shown, leaving ½ in wide strip. Appliqué (p10) this strip on top of the pieced panels, making sure that qppliqué strip lines up with the bottom of light blue arc.

9 Sew pieced arc to top of panel C,

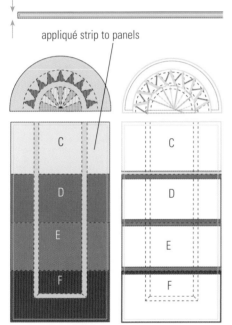

appliqué strip to panels

pressing seam toward panel. Cut loop 1 in x 2½ in from orange scrap. Fold long sides in ¼ in on both sides, press. Fold pressed strip in half again, creating ¼ in x 2½ in piece. Stitch along the side with matching thread.

Place both ends, side by side, on top of the center of the pieced arc. Sew in place with ¼ in seam allowance.

10 Embroider wild grass (p110) onto appliqué panels, as shown.

11 Make trim from 3 different orange and yellow fabrics by cutting 14 bias cut pieces 1 in x 3 in for a total of 42 pieces. Sew these pieces together, alternating colors, at a 45° angle. Press the pieced trim strip in half, lengthwise, wrong sides together. Place trim onto top of cover, raw edges of trim even with raw edges of cover. Sew through 2 layers of trim and the cover with ¼ in seam allowance. Overlap 2 ends of trim and hand sew in place.

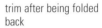

sew trim on top of cover r.s.t. around outside edge

make loop for top of tote
top view w.s.

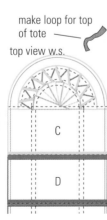

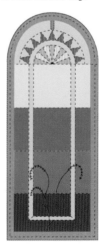

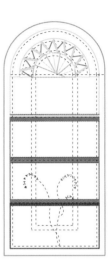

trim after being folded back

w.s. view of back with trim folded out before stitching it to the back

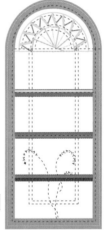

stitch trim to back of cover with ¼ in s.a.

12 Make fabric button (pattern p110), cut 2 pieces from orange fabric scrap. Place right sides together and sew with narrow seam allowance, leaving a small section unstitched. Turn right side out and sew opening closed. Roll up (wide side to point) forming a fabric button, and sew point in place using matching thread. Fabric button will be stitched to the top cover in the center of the E and F panel after tote is assembled.

Lining

13 Cut one lining from light blue fabric and one batting using pattern p108. Place lining right side up on top of batting and stitch together around the outer edge with a very narrow seam allowance. This piece is now ready for the pockets.

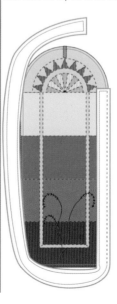

Pockets

1 Make templates for all pockets (patterns p110). Cut pockets from cream felt.

 Note All pocket pieces are cut the finished size.

2 Project pocket P1

Cut 4 pieces cream felt P1 (see diagrams P1, p109). With variegated embroidery floss, blanket stitch around outer edge of three P1 pieces. Stitch remaining P1 piece in place on light blue lining with blanket stitch around entire outer edge. (See pockets placement guide below.). On front of one P1 piece, embroider stem stitch stems with 2 strands variegated brown thread, fly stitch for leaves in green and French knots for flowers using variegated orange/brown. This piece is the top flap below. Assemble all prepared pocket pieces P1 by placing one on top of the other and blanket stitch through all four pockets along one side (check dotted line on placement guide) to form a book. These pages can be used to hold fabric shapes in place.

3 Pencil pocket P2 &P3. Cut 2 pieces cream felt (P2 &P3) (see pattern P110). Fold top down 1 in and embroider wild grass stems (stem stitch) with 2 strands of variegated brown, catching folded down

Pockets placement guide

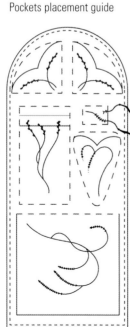

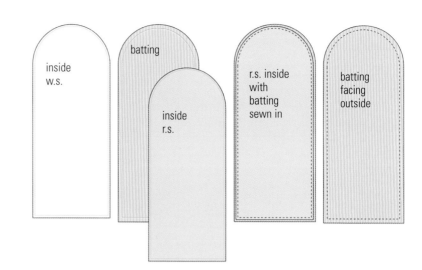

inside
w.s.

batting

inside
r.s.

r.s. inside
with
batting
sewn in

batting
facing
outside

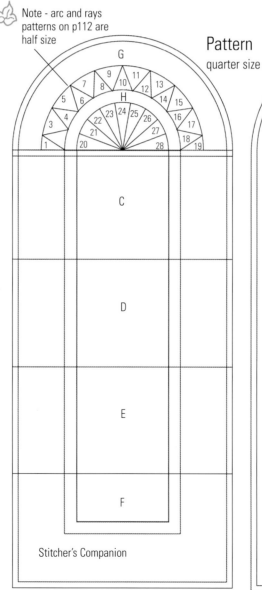

Note - arc and rays patterns on p112 are half size

Pattern

quarter size

G

7 8 9 10 11 12 13 14 15

5 6 H 16

3 4 23 24 25 26 17

22 21 27 18

1 20 28 19

C

D

E

F

Stitcher's Companion

Stitcher's Companion

Pocket Directions

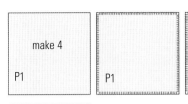

make 4

P1

P1

P1 cover

P1-1 is the back and P1-2 is the cover. Stitch a blanket stitch around edges of 3 pieces. Embroider the top flap before stitching the pieces together

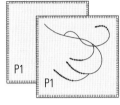

P1

P1

P1

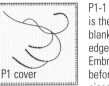

P5

P5 – thimble pocket - make pleats as indicated by the half circles for the thimble

P4 – needle case & pin cushion

needle case

embroider a blanket stich around 2 of the outer edges

needle case and pin cushion

place batting between outer pieces & embroider a blanket stich around the edge

P4   P4

P4   P4

batting

P4   P4   batting

outside

outside

lay batting on top of both outer casings

sew both casings together with batting inside with a blanket stitch on the raw edge

P2 & P3 – pencil pocket

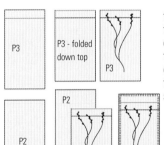

P3

P3 - folded down top

P3

P3

fold the top of P3 & embroider the grass over the top fold to secure it

P2

P2

P3

P2 & 3

Lay P3 on top of P2 and stitch the 2 together to the lining with a blanket stitch

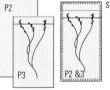

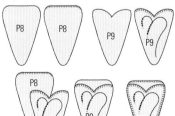

P8   P8

P9   P9

P8

P9   P9

P9 – blanket stitch around top arches & embroider grass

P6 & P7 – needle case & pin cushion pockets embroider a blanket stitch along the curved edges

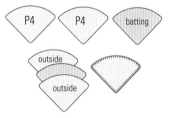

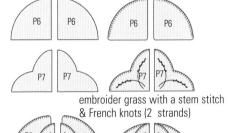

P6   P6

P6   P6

P7   P7

P7   P7

P6   P6

P7   P7

embroider grass with a stem stitch & French knots (2 strands)

stitch together P6 & P7 to the lining with a blanket stitch along the straight edges

edge with embroidery stitch. Leaves are green lazy daisy stitches and flowers of French knots using orange/brown variegated threads (see instructions diagram, p110). Place embroidered P2 on top of P3 and place on light blue lining (check placement guide) and blanket stitch in place through all layers.

4 Needle case and pin cushion P4 (see pattern p110). For needle case, cut 2 pieces from both the cream felt and cotton batting (see directions diagram p109). Lay batting on top of both outer felt pieces. Embroider a blanket stitch around the curved edge and one straight edge. Place stitched pieces together with batting pages on the inside and blanket stitch along raw edge, joining both pieces together. Batting pages will hold all your needles. For pincushion cut 2 pieces from both cream felt and 1 from cotton batting (see diagram on p110). Place batting piece between the two felt pieces and embroider a blanket stitch around outer edge.

5 Needle and Pincushion pockets P6 & P7 (instruction diagram on p109). Cut 2 pieces each of P6 and P7 from cream felt. Using 2 strands of floss embroider grass on the 2 P7 pieces with a stem stitch using variegated brown thread, lazy daisy stitch with green thread for leaves, and French knots for flower using orange/brown thread. Blanket stitch the top edges of arcs of each P7 piece using 2 strands of variegated brown floss. Place the P7 pieces on top of P6 pieces. Position onto light blue lining (check placement diagram, p108), and blanket stitch in place around all outer edges.

6 Thimble Holder P5 (see pattern, p110). Cut one P5 from cream felt. Embroider grass with 6 strands of

Tote Patterns
half size

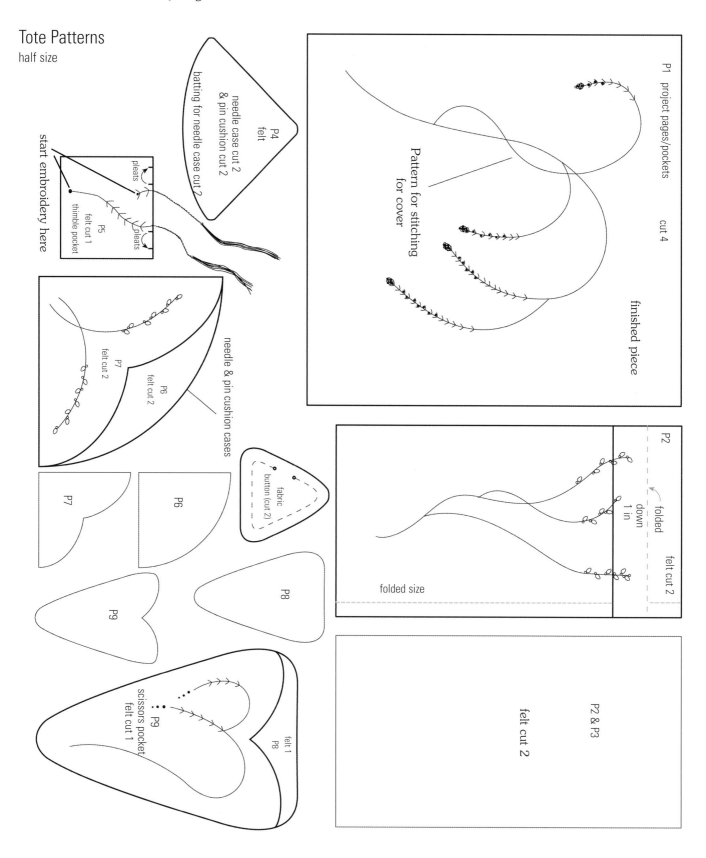

P1 project pages/pockets   cut 4   finished piece

Pattern for stitching
for cover

needle case cut 2
& pin cushion cut 2
batting for needle case cut 2

P4
felt

start embroidery here

pleats

P5
felt cut 1
thimble pocket

pleats

P7
felt cut 2

P6
felt cut 2

needle & pin cushion cases

P7

P6

fabric
button (cut 2)

P9

P8

P9
scissors pocket
felt cut 1

felt 1
P8

P2
folded
down
1 in
felt cut 2

folded size

P2 & P3
felt cut 2

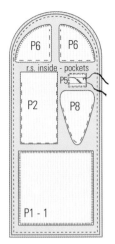

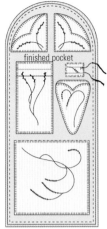

stitch the first part to the lining

stitch all the pockets in place

variegated embroidery thread starting at the bottom of each stem. Leave a long tail of thread at the top of the pocket on each stem. Braid these long threads for 1½ in, tie a knot and leave the remaining threads to form a tassel. Place a few fly stitches with brown and green embroidery thread along each stem. Pleat the bottom of the thimble pocket, and pin to hold in place. Blanket stitch the top edge of pocket, then position thimble pocket onto light blue lining (see placement diagram, p108) and blanket stitch the remaining three sides, making sure to keep bottom edge pleated as you stitch. The top will be open to hold

your thimble and the tassels can be tied into a bow to secure your precious thimble.

7 Scissor pocket P8 and P9 - cut one P8 and one P9 from cream felt. Embroider grass stems onto P9 with stem stitch using 2 strands brown variegated thread, green thread for leaves, and orange/brown thread for French knot flowers. Blanket stitch around top arc of P9 with 2 strands variegated brown thread. Place P9 on top of P8, positon onto light blue lining, and blanket stitch in place (see placement diagram p109) around the outer edges. The top of P9 will be left open to form the pocket for your favorite scissors.

8 Assemble Tote (See p111 diagrams).

Layer finished sections (pockets on lining and tote cover) by placing them right sides together. Stitch around the outer edge with ¼ in seam allowance, leaving bottom edge open. Turn right side out and hand stitch the bottom edge using matching colored thread. Sew fabric button in place and insert the needle case and pin cushion.

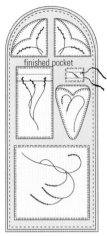

view of w.s. of outer tote cover r.s.t. with the pocket lining

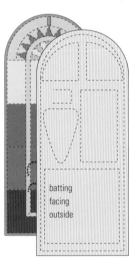

place the outer tote cover and inside pocket lining r.s.t. with the batting facing outside

stitch together the outer tote and the pocket lining leaving the bottom open

turn right side out and stitch the bottom edge close

inside of tote complete with needle case and pin cushion ready to go into their pockets

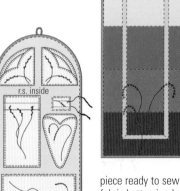

piece ready to sew fabric button in place

Pattern – G, H, arc & rays
half size

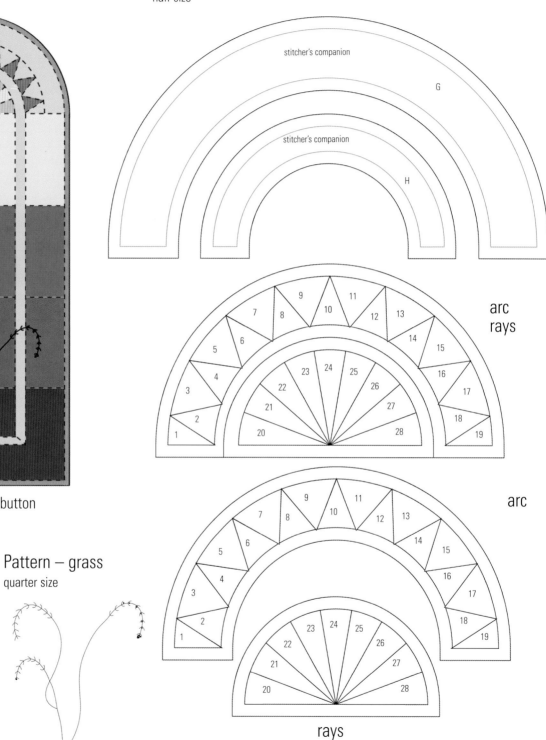

stitcher's companion

G

stitcher's companion

H

arc
rays

arc

rays

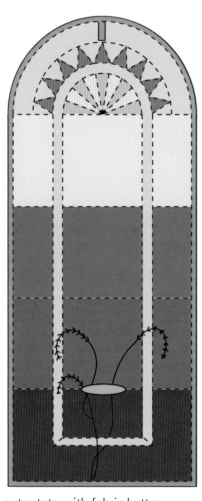

outer tote with fabric button

Pattern – grass
quarter size

Autumn Friendship Mini Quilt

Materials

- background cream fabric ¼ yd
- basket & spool thread blue fabric 6 in sq
- basket & spool thread green fabric 6 in sq
- trees green print 4 in sq
- house gray print 6 in sq
- hands pink fabric 4 in sq
- roof, door, chimney setting strips, and binding black fabric ⅛ yd
- hearts red fabric 5 in sq
- spool ends tan fabric 3 in x 5 in
- stars and window yellow fabric 5 in sq
- embroidery threads

This miniature quilt is a scaled-down version of a full-size quilt, allowing for experimentation of design and color without investing a lot of time. Years ago, when I was teaching at a Quilt Retreat, everyone gave me scraps of fabric to create a little quilt in memory of the event. The house is the meeting place, surrounded by trees and stars, with helping/sharing hands, baskets to hold treasures, and spools of thread everywhere. This friendship quilt is hand pieced (p8) and appliquéd (p11) with some embroidery (p16). Finished size is 10 ¼ in x 8 ¾ in.

Note Because of the size of the individual pieces, hand piecing is recommended.

Directions

Photocopy pattern (p119) to full size, cover with a sheet of freezer paper (p8) and completely trace each piece. These are templates. Mark all pieces. Cut out. Use to make each section of quilt .

 Note All templates from A to W add ¼ in seam allowance before cutting fabric See Hand Piecing, p8.

Stars

1 To make one block, trace around templates A and B on designated cream and yellow fabrics with sharp pencil. Allow ¼ in extra on every side for seam allowance. Cut out.

use pattern p119 to trace A & B

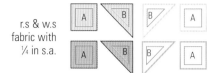

r.s & w.s fabric with ¼ in s.a.

Cream – Cut 4 A and 4 B.
Yellow – Cut 1 A and 4 B.

2 Sew triangle cream to triangle yellow. Sew 3 squares together. Press towards yellow. Repeat to make 3 rows.

 Note Press in direction of blue arrows

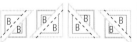

w.s. view cream is pressed toward yellow

3 Assemble rows 1, 2, and 3. Press seams, as shown. Sew rows together and press, as shown in diagram.

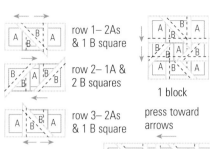

row 1– 2As & 1 B square

row 2– 1A & 2 B squares

row 3– 2As & 1 B square

1 block

press toward arrows

4 Repeat steps 1 to 3 to make a second block. Sew the 2 blocks together.

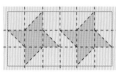 *Note* All row seams must be pressed in the opposite direction.

2 blocks r.s view

Star section should measure 3½ in x 2 in.

Meeting House

1 To make one block, trace around templates C to L on designated fabrics with sharp pencil. Allow ¼ in seam allowance on every side. Cut out.

Cream – Cut 2 C, 1 E, 1 F, and 1 H.

Black – Cut 2 D, 1 G, and 1 L.

Yellow – Cut 1 K.

House print – Cut 1 I, 2 J, 2 K, and 2 L. See pattern, p119.

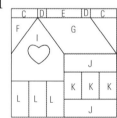

use pattern p121 to trace C, D, E, F, G, H, I, J, K, & L

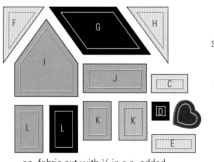

r.s. fabric cut with ¼ in s.a. added

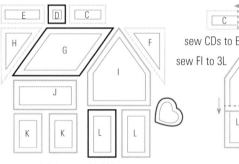

w.s. fabric cut with ¼ in s.a.

2 Assemble in sections, as shown. (diagrams - arrows indicate seam pressing directions.)

 Note Press in direction of blue arrows.

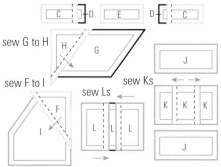

sew Cs to Ds

sew G to H

sew F to I

sew Ls

sew Ks

sew 2C2DE to rest of house

sew CDs to E

sew FI to 3L

sew Js to 3K

sew FI3L to GH

3 Sew chimney section to top of roof section. Press seams towards side and towards roof at the top. House block measures 3½ in x 3½ in.

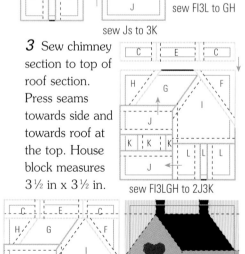

sew FI3LGH to 2J3K

r.s. house pieced together

Tree

1 To make one block, trace around templates M to Q on designated fabrics with sharp pencil. Allow ¼ in extra on all sides for seam allowance Cut out. Assemble tree block as shown.
Green – Cut 1 O.
Cream – Cut 1 M, 1 N, and 2 P.
Brown – Cut 1 Q.

use pattern p121 to trace M, N, O, P & Q

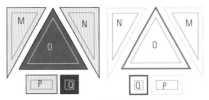

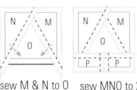

r.s. & w.s. fabric cut with ¼ in s.a.

2 Sew M & N to each side of O. Sew one P to each side of Q.

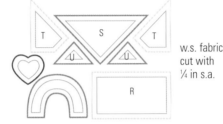

sew M & N to O   sew MNO to 2PQ

sew Ps to Q

3 Sew pieced units together and press. Make 2 blocks and stitch together, as shown. Tree block should measure 2 in x 3½ in.

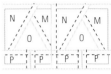

blocks w.s. view

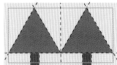

tree blocks r.s. view

Gathering Basket

1 To make one block, trace around templates R to U on designated fabrics with sharp pencil. Allow ¼ in extra for seam allowance on all sides. Cut out. Assemble basket as shown.
Cream – Cut 1 R and 2 T.
Blue – Cut 1 S and 2 U, and 1 for the handle.
Green - Cut 1 S, and 2 U, and 1 for the handle.
See fusible applique, p11.

use pattern p121 to trace R, S, T, U & handle

r.s. fabric cut with ¼ in s.a.

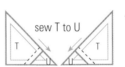

w.s. fabric cut with ¼ in s.a.

2 Appliqué handle to R piece, making sure to bring bottom edges of handle to edge of R to be included in the seam.

sew handle to R   r.s. & w.s views

3 Sew U pieces to bottom of T pieces. Press. Stitch T/U units to each side of S. Stitch R section to STU unit. Press in direction of arrows.

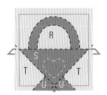

sew T to U

sew 2TU to S

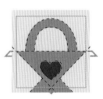

sew R/handle unit to STU unit w.s. & r.s views

4 Stitch 2 rows together and press. Repeat for second block using green instead of blue fabric. Block should measure 2½ in x 2½ in. (Heart is added later.)

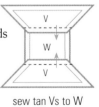

r.s green basket

Spool

1 To make one block, trace around templates V and W on designated fabrics with a sharp pencil. Allow ¼ in extra for seam allowance on all sides. Cut out. Assemble spool block as shown.
Cream – Cut 2 V
Tan – Cut 2 V
Blue – Cut 1 W
Green – Cut 1 W

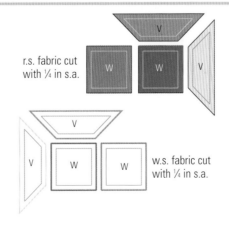

use pattern p121 to trace R, S, T, U & handle

r.s. fabric cut with ¼ in s.a.

w.s. fabric cut with ¼ in s.a.

2 Sew 2 V tan pieces to blue W. Press towards W.

3 Set in the 2 V cream pieces. Press towards spool ends and thread.

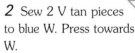

sew tan Vs to W

sew cream Vs to W

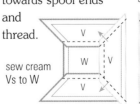

4 Repeat to make a second block using green W fabric piece. Block should measure 2½ in x 2½ in.

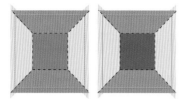

r.s. views of blue & green spools

Hearts

1 Make template of heart. Trace on designated fabric with a sharp pencil. Make 5. Allow ¼ in extra for seam allowance on all sides. Cut out.
2 Appliqué one on each basket, one on each hand, and one on house. See pattern p119.

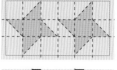

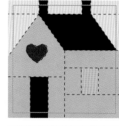

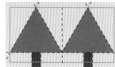

r.s. views of middle sections stars, house & trees to be stitched together

Helping Hands

1 To make one block, trace templates for hands on designated fabric with a sharp pencil. Allow ¼ in extra for seam allowance on all sides. Cut out. Assemble hands block as shown. Cream – Cut one 2½ in x 2½ in square. Pink – Cut 2 hands (make sure hands make 1 pair).

use pattern p121 to trace hands

r.s..fabric cut with ¼ in s.a.

2 Needle-turn appliqué (p10) the hand to the center of the 2½ in x 2½ in cream square.

Note An alternative method is fusible appliqué (p11).
3 Repeat to make second block. Each hand block measures 2½ in x 2½ in.

r.s. views of right & left hands

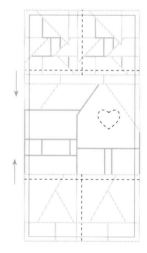

diagram simplified

w.s. view of middle section – stitch and press in direction of arrows

Assemble Quilt Top

1 Assemble pieced blocks in verticle rows.
Row 1 Blue thread Spool black/Helping Hands/Green Basket
Row 2 Stars/Meeting House/Trees
Row 3 Green thread Spool black/Helping Hands/Blue Basket

r.s. views of outer sections spools, hands & baskets to be stitched together

Row 1   Row 3

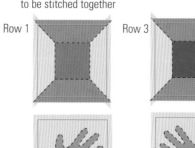

w.s. view of outer sections – stitch and press in direction of arrows

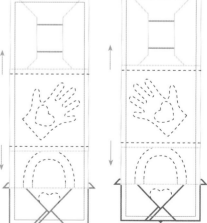

1 To make setting strips and small black border: Black – Cut two ¾ in x 6½ in setting strips, two ¾ in x 8 in top and bottom border, and two ¾ in x 7 in side borders.

pressing guide - press in direction of arrows

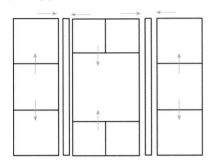

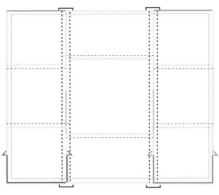

w.s. view of all sections & black setting strips in place to stitch together – press in direction of arrows

2 Mark ¼ in seam allowance on each strip and sew setting strips between vertical rows.

Note Finished strip is ¼ in wide making it crucial to sew as straight as possible

Press towards strips.

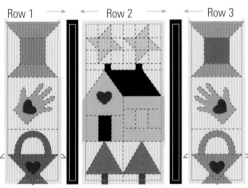

r.s. view of all sections & black setting strips in place to stitch together – press in direction of arrows

diagrams simplified

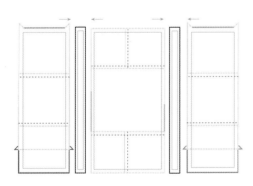

w.s. view of all sections & black setting strips in place to stitch together – press in direction of arrows

r.s. of all sections & black setting strips stitched in place & ready for inside top & bottom black borders – press in direction of arrows

3 Sew top and bottom borders. Press towards black border. Piece should measure 8½ in x 7 in.
4 Sew side borders. Piece should measure 8½ in x 7 in.

5 To make outer border cut 2 cream 8½ in x 1½ in top and bottom border, cut two 8¾ in x 1½ in side borders.
6 Sew on top and bottom borders with ¼ in seam allowance. Press towards black border. Piece should measure 8½ in x 8¾ in.

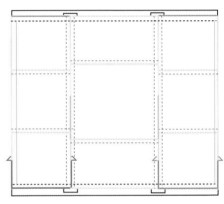

w.s. view of sections , setting strips & inside black top & bottom borders sewn together

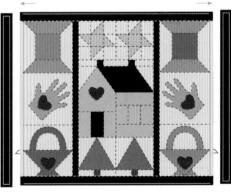

r.s. of section with inside top & bottom black borders stitched & ready for inside black borders

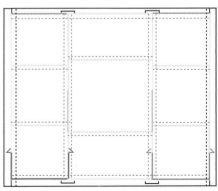

w.s of sections & all inside black borders sewn together

r.s. of sections with inside black borders stitched in & ready for top & bottom cream outer borders – press in direction of arrows

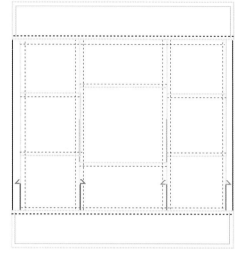

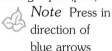

w.s. of inside black bordered section & cream top & bottom outer borders sewn together

r.s. of black inner border section with top & bottom cream outer borders stitched in & ready for side cream outer borders – press in direction of arrows

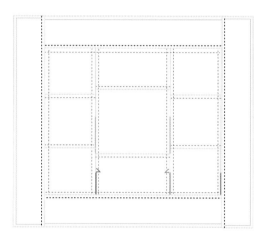

w.s. of black bordered section & cream outer borders sewn together

7 Sew on side borders. Press towards black border. Piece should measure 8 ¾ in x 10 ½ in.

8 To finish, add embroidery stitches to spools and the words in the border with back stitch, stem stitch, and French knots.

9 Layer the quilt and quilt (p12) around images. Bind (p13) and sign quilt (p15).

Note Press in direction of blue arrows

embroider thread on spools & around hands with a 2 strand thread with a stem stitch

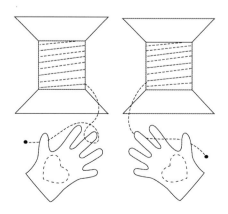

laughter
sharing
friends
family

Spools & Hands
half size

Words
half size

embroider words with a 2 strand thread with a back stitch & French knots

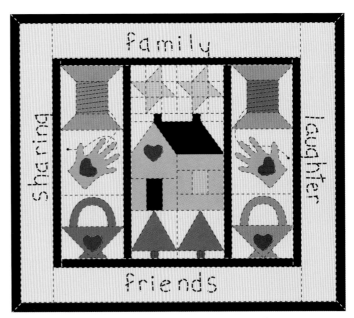

r.s. of quilt top with outer cream outer borders stitched in
& ready for binding

finished mini quilt

Pattern

half size

Patchwork Fan & Heart
Toss Cushions

Materials
Fan Cushion
- A to F pieces
  (6 different varieties)
  plain or print cream
  and taupe fabric
  5 in x 9 in
- G piece plain or print
  cream or taupe fabric
  5 ½ in x 5 in
- H piece plain or print
  cream or taupe fabric
  8 in x 18 in
- poly stuffing
- beads
- embroidery threads
- Cluny lace 4 yds

Heart Cushion
- foundation piece
  12 in x 15 in
- cotton pieces in cream
  and taupe
- backing 12 in x 16 in
- poly stuffing
- embroidery threads
- beads
- Cluny lace 3 ¼ yds

These beautiful cushions show off all your fancy needlework accenting autumn themes. The fan cushion is approximately 14 in x 16 in and the Patchwork Heart Toss Cushion is 12 in x 16 in including lace. Directions and pattern for Heart Toss Cushion, p39, p123.

Directions

1 Make 6 templates (p8) for fan pieces (pattern this page). Seam allowance is ¼ in. Place template on fabric and cut ¼ in seam allowance around the outside edges of templates.

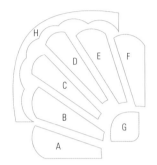

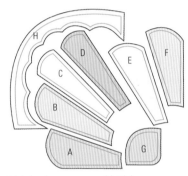

cut fabric pieces r.s. up with ¹/₄ in s.a.

2 Sew wedges together (A to B to C, etc). Press in direction of arrows.

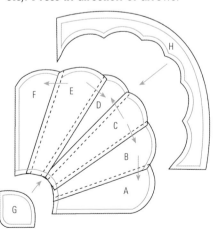

3 Sew G over top of pieced wedge unit. Sew H over top of pieced wedge.

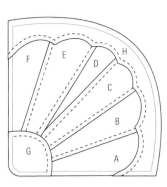

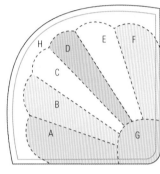

4 Embroider pieced fan top using these stitches: stem, satin, straight (couched in place), blanket, button hole with French knots and feather. Sew beads to the end of each feather stitch. See embroidery patterns under fan cushion, p123.

5 Place backing right sides together with pieced fan cushion top and sew ¼ in seam allowance around the edge leaving a 3 in gap.

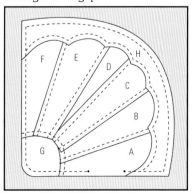

Pattern - Fan
quarter size

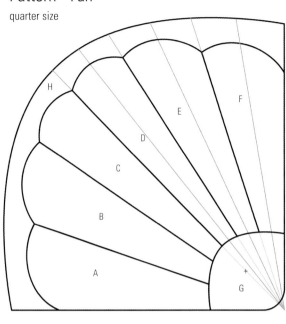

6 Trim backing and turn right side out.

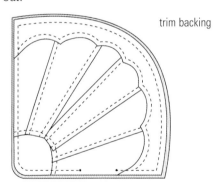

trim backing

7 Fill with poly stuffing and stitch the opening closed. Sew Cluny lace on as instructed, p41.

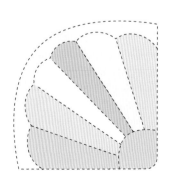

finished fan toss cushion ready for lace

Crazy Patch Greeting Card

Materials
- handmade paper cards (any size)
- matching envelopes
- quilting scraps
- embroidery thread

This beautiful card emphasizes autumn themes with fall colors and embroidery motifs.

Stitches – refer to embroidery diagram p16 to choose your own stitches or cover the seams or you can refer to the photo as a guide.

Directions

See Winter Heart Toss cushion p40 for patchwork technique. Use two strands of embroidery floss for your stitches.

Pumpkin

Stem – stem stitch.

Leaves – stem stitch outline and fill in with satin stitch.

Tendrils – outline with stem stitch

Pumpkin – stem stitch outline and fill in with satin stitch.

Pumpkin

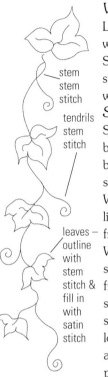

leaves – outline with stem stitch & fill in with satin stitch

tendrils – stem stitch

stem – outline with stem stitch & fill in with satin stitch

pumpkin – outline with stem stitch & fill in with satin stitch

Embroidery Patterns for fan & heart cushion – Draped flower, Spider & Web, Grapes, Pumpkin, Vine quarter size

Vine

Leaves – outline with stem stitch.

Stem– outline with stem stitch and fill in with satin stitch.

Spider and Web

Spider – a bugle bead is used for the body, the legs are straight stitches

Web - stem stitch lines radiating out from center point.

Web is filled with straight stitches from the longest spike to the shorter spike to the next longest, etc. and are anchored at each point with a back stitch to secure it. Spider trailing line is back stitched with 1 strand

stem stem stitch

tendrils stem stitch

leaves – outline with stem stitch & fill in with satin stitch

embroidery thread.

Draped flower

The stems are stitched with a stem stitch. the flowers are

made with fly stitches and French knots.

Grapes

Fruit – stem stitch outline and fill in with satin stitch.

tendrils – stem stitch outline.

leaves – stem stitch outline and fill in with satin stitch.

stem – stem stitch outline and fill in with satin stitch.

Spider & Web

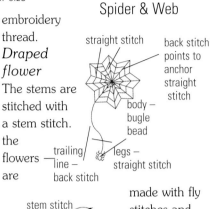

straight stitch

back stitch points to anchor straight stitch

body – bugle bead

legs – straight stitch

trailing line – back stitch

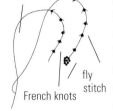

stem stitch

French knots

fly stitch

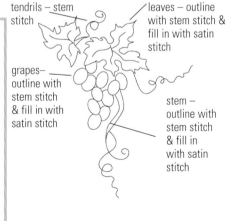

tendrils – stem stitch

grapes– outline with stem stitch & fill in with satin stitch

leaves – outline with stem stitch & fill in with satin stitch

stem – outline with stem stitch & fill in with satin stitch

Autumn Crazy Patch Greeting Card

Pattern three quarter size

Directions

Cut out oval. See instructions on p43 for piecing and assembly in Winter Crazy Patch Greeting Cards. See diagram for embroidery stitches used and refer to embroidery diagrams p16 for technique or refer to photo as a guide. Use single strand embroidery floss for your stitches.

Birds– feather stitch

Pine trees needles – straight stitch

Tree trunks – stem stitch

Wheat stems– stem stitch.

Wheat leaves – 2 lazy daisy stitches,

Kernels – fly stitch.

Optional - along a couple of seams you can add cretan stitches.

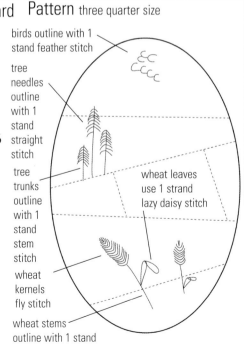

birds outline with 1 stand feather stitch

tree needles outline with 1 stand straight stitch

tree trunks outline with 1 stand stem stitch

wheat kernels fly stitch

wheat stems outline with 1 stand stem stitch

wheat leaves use 1 strand lazy daisy stitch

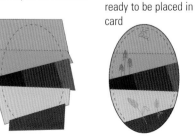

piece ready to be trimmed

embroidered piece ready to be placed in card

Crazy Patchwork
Scrappy Bear

Materials

- muslin ⅓ yd
- various color cotton scraps from patchwork and 2 small pieces for ears
- velvet for head/ears, foot pads
- poly stuffing
- buttons for eyes and attaching arms and legs
- doll-making needle for attaching arms and legs
- ribbon tie

This delightful bear is made from leftover scraps from the autumn projects. It can sit or stand anywhere and is a charming accent to fall decor.

Directions

Cut out pattern pieces as indicated on p127. Cut 1 pair pattern A from velvet fabric for ears and 1 pair velvet head side pieces pattern B.

Patchwork bear

Cover each foundation piece D-E using the crazy patch method p40. Trim all scrap pieces to the edges making all even with the foundation piece.

Ear

1 Sew the ears, 1 velvet with 1 muslin, right sides together around outer edge. See p126 A.

2 Turn right side out. Stuff lightly with poly stuffing.

3 Turn bottom edge in ¼ in and baste. Slip stitch front to back and form 2 pleats, as shown, p126.

Head

1 Sew darts on side head pieces.

2 Sew side head pieces together from dot on nose to neck edge, as shown. Press seems open.

3 Sew center head C to side head unit, matching dot and neck edges.

4 Turn head right side out.

5 Turn neck edge under ¼ in and baste.

6 Stuff head firmly and slip stitch ears in place, as shown.

Body

1 Sew fronts together, as shown.

2 Sew backs together, as shown.

3 Sew back and front together along the sides, leaving top (neck edge) open.

4 Turn neck edge over ¼ in and baste, as shown.

5 Stuff body, leaving about 2 in unstuffed at the top which will be stuffed after head is attached

Arms

1 Sew velvet pads to inner arm. Press sides open.

2 Sew inner arms to outer arm, leaving open between dots.

3 Turn right sides out, stuff, sew opening closed.

Legs

1 Sew legs together in pairs, stitching from dot to dot and leaving lower edge unstitched, as shown.

2 Sew foot soles to lower edge of legs, matching the dots with the seams. Turn right side out. Stuff and sew opening closed.

Assemble Bear

1 Slip stitch head to body, making sure to line up center head seam with center body seam. Sew, leaving 1½ to 2 in opening. Stuff more filling into the body and neck area, so head will stay upright. Sew remaining seam closed.

2 Attach arms and legs with strong thread and buttons. Using long doll-making needles, stitch right through the bear's body.

3 Sew buttons in position for the eyes.

4 Using 3 strands of black embroidery floss, embroider nose with satin stitch. Back stitch the mouth. See photo.

5 Add a satin ribbon around the bear's neck.

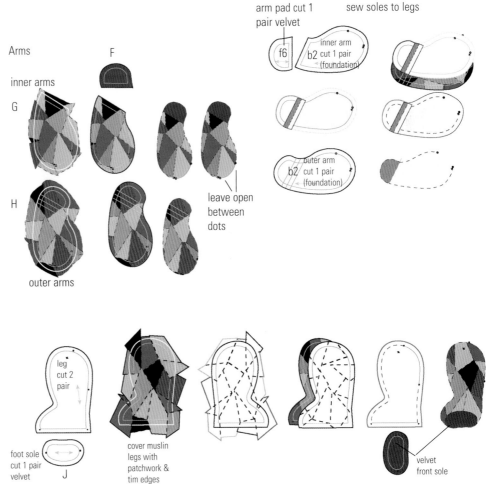

arm pad cut 1 pair velvet
sew soles to legs
f6
inner arm b2 cut 1 pair (foundation)
outer arm b2 cut 1 pair (foundation)
Arms
inner arms
F
G
H
outer arms
leave open between dots
leg cut 2 pair
foot sole cut 1 pair velvet   J
cover muslin legs with patchwork & tim edges
velvet front sole

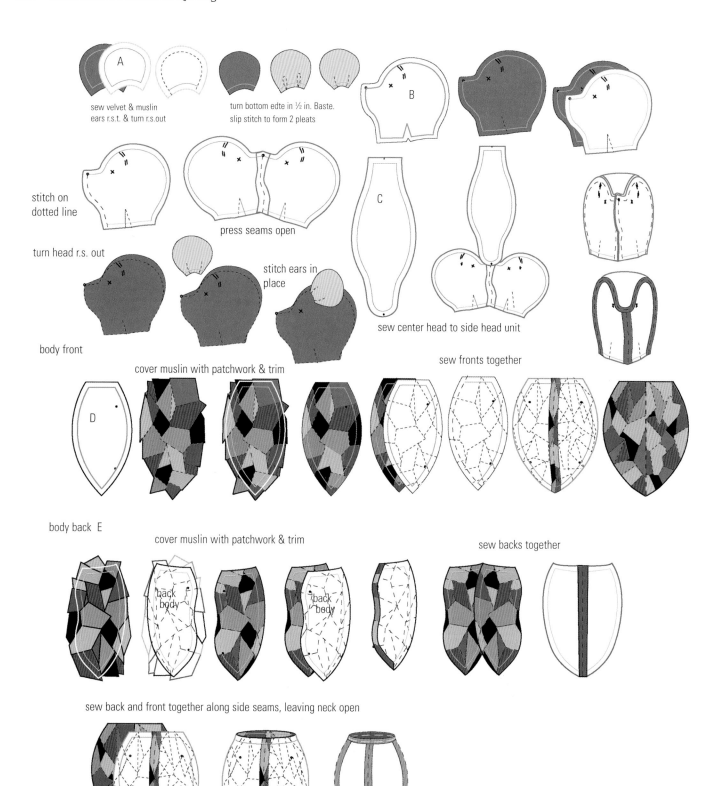

sew velvet & muslin
ears r.s.t. & turn r.s.out

turn bottom edte in ½ in. Baste.
slip stitch to form 2 pleats

A

B

stitch on
dotted line

press seams open

turn head r.s. out

C

stitch ears in
place

body front

sew center head to side head unit

cover muslin with patchwork & trim

sew fronts together

D

body back E

cover muslin with patchwork & trim

sew backs together

back
body

back
body

sew back and front together along side seams, leaving neck open

wrong side out

Patterns

half size

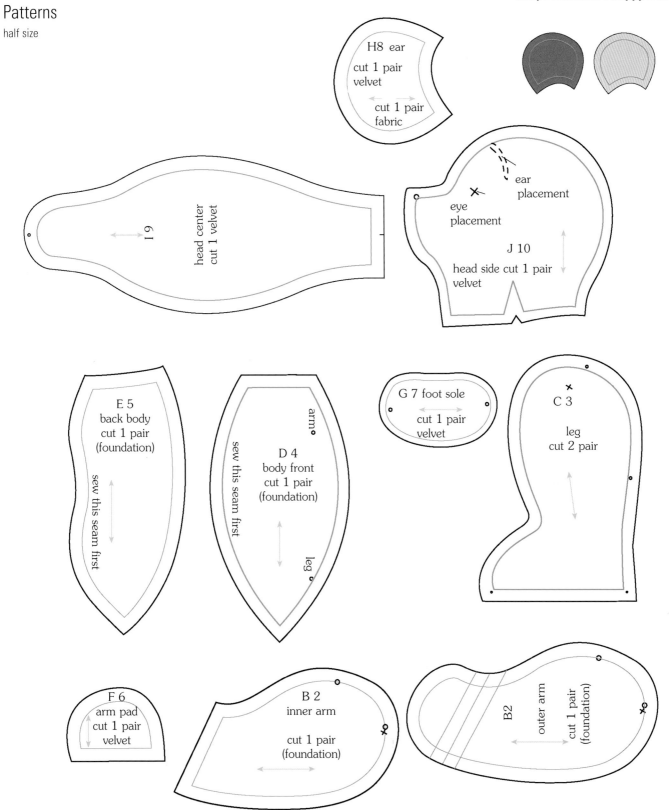

H8 ear
cut 1 pair
velvet

cut 1 pair
fabric

head center
cut 1 velvet

I 9

ear
placement

eye
placement

J 10

head side cut 1 pair
velvet

E 5
back body
cut 1 pair
(foundation)

sew this seam first

D 4
body front
cut 1 pair
(foundation)

sew this seam first

arm

leg

G 7 foot sole
cut 1 pair
velvet

C 3

leg
cut 2 pair

F 6
arm pad
cut 1 pair
velvet

B 2
inner arm

cut 1 pair
(foundation)

B2

outer arm

cut 1 pair
(foundation)

Index

Metric Conversion Chart MM=Millemeters CM=Centimeters				
Inches	MM	CM	Inches	CM
1/8	3	0.3	4	10.2
1/4	6	0.6	4½	11.4
3/8	10	1.0	5	12.7
1/2	13	1.3	6	15.2
5/8	16	1.6	7	17.8
3/4	19	1.9	8	20.3
7/8	22	22.2	9	22.9
1	25	2.5	10	25.4
1¼	32	3.2	11	27.9
1½	38	3.8	12	30.5
1¾	44	4.4	13	33.0
2	51	5.1	14	35.6
2½	64	6.4	15	38.1
3	76	7.6	16	40.6
3½	89	8.9		